D1257784

A GUIDE TO ONLINE COURSE DESIGN

**FREE
Premium Content**
▼

JB
JOSSEY-BASS™
A Wiley Brand

This book includes premium content that can be
accessed from our Web site when you register at
www.josseybass.com/go/stavredes_herder
using the password **josseybasshighereducation**.

A GUIDE TO ONLINE COURSE DESIGN

STRATEGIES FOR STUDENT SUCCESS

Tina Stavredes and Tiffany Herder

JB JOSSEY-BASS™

A Wiley Brand

Cover design by Michael Cook

Copyright © 2014 by John Wiley & Sons, Inc. All rights reserved.

Published by Jossey-Bass
A Wiley Brand
One Montgomery Street, Suite 1200, San Francisco, CA 94104-4594—www.josseybass.com

No part of this publication may be reproduced, stored in a retrieval system, or transmitted in any form or by
any means, electronic, mechanical, photocopying, recording, scanning, or otherwise, except as permitted
under Section 107 or 108 of the 1976 United States Copyright Act, without either the prior written permission
of the publisher, or authorization through payment of the appropriate per-copy fee to the Copyright Clearance
Center, Inc., 222 Rosewood Drive, Danvers, MA 01923, 978-750-8400, fax 978-646-8600, or on the Web at
www.copyright.com. Requests to the publisher for permission should be addressed to the Permissions
Department, John Wiley & Sons, Inc., 111 River Street, Hoboken, NJ 07030, 201-748-6011, fax 201-748-6008,
or online at www.wiley.com/go/permissions.

Limit of Liability/Disclaimer of Warranty: While the publisher and author have used their best efforts in
preparing this book, they make no representations or warranties with respect to the accuracy or completeness
of the contents of this book and specifically disclaim any implied warranties of merchantability or fitness for a
particular purpose. No warranty may be created or extended by sales representatives or written sales materials.
The advice and strategies contained herein may not be suitable for your situation. You should consult with a
professional where appropriate. Neither the publisher nor author shall be liable for any loss of profit or any
other commercial damages, including but not limited to special, incidental, consequential, or other damages.
Readers should be aware that Internet websites offered as citations and/or sources for further information may
have changed or disappeared between the time this was written and when it is read.

Jossey-Bass books and products are available through most bookstores. To contact Jossey-Bass directly call our
Customer Care Department within the U.S. at 800-956-7739, outside the U.S. at 317-572-3986, or fax
317-572-4002.

Wiley publishes in a variety of print and electronic formats and by print-on-demand. Some material included
with standard print versions of this book may not be included in e-books or in print-on-demand. If this book
refers to media such as a CD or DVD that is not included in the version you purchased, you may download this
material at http://booksupport.wiley.com. For more information about Wiley products, visit www.wiley.com.

Library of Congress Cataloging-in-Publication Data has been applied for and is on file with the Library of
Congress.

ISBN 978-1-118-46266-9 (paper); ISBN 978-1-118-79138-7 (ebk); ISBN 978-1-118-79139-4 (ebk)

Printed in the United States of America
FIRST EDITION

PB Printing   10 9 8 7 6 5 4 3 2 1

The Jossey-Bass Higher
and Adult Education Series

This book is dedicated to our husbands, Jim Stavredes and Jason Herder, who provided endless encouragement and support throughout the writing of this book.

Contents

Exhibits and Figures

EXHIBITS

FIGURES

Preface

The 2010 online learning survey in *Changing Course* (Allen & Seaman, 2010) reveals that enrollment in online courses rose by almost one million learners from a year earlier. The survey of more than 2,500 colleges and universities nationwide finds approximately 5.6 million learners were enrolled in at least one online course during fall 2009. The report indicates that nearly 30 percent of all college and university students now take at least one course online. In addition, the report also implies that there may be problems ahead. Although the sluggish economy continues to drive enrollment growth, large public institutions are feeling budget pressure and competition from the for-profit sector institutions. Additionally, the 2010 Sloan survey shows that three-quarters of polled institutions report that the economic downturn has increased demand for online courses and programs.

According to research comparing online course development approaches between 2001 and 2006 (Green, 2010), the individual instructor approach was by far the most widely used approach to course development. Seventy percent of the respondents indicated they developed online courses on their own in 2006, which is a rise from previous years. Other studies indicate that instructors continue to be responsible for designing online courses, and many in the absence of an instructional design specialist (Barker, 2002; Kozlowski, 2004; Mills, Fisher, & Stair, 2001; O'Neill, 1998). Surveys conducted by Brogden and Couros (2002),

Grosse (2004), and Lorenzetti (2004) suggest that the time and effort demands to develop online courses and to learn new technologies causes faculty member frustrations. Rockwell, Schauer, Fritz, and Marx (1999) evaluated the types of knowledge and support faculty members felt were needed to be successful in online course development. Faculty members responded that they need training to develop effective instructional materials and interactive elements for the online environment. The literature reflects that many online faculty members learn the instructional design fundamentals through trial and error in their online experiences rather than through formal instruction (Link & Scholtz, 2000; Oblinger & Hawkins, 2006; Pankowski, 2008; Ryan, Carlton, & Ali, 2004; Schrum, 2002). However, developing and delivering effective online courses requires pedagogy and technology expertise possessed by few faculty members. Online instruction is more than a series of readings posted to a website; it requires deliberate instructional design that hinges on linking learning objectives to specific learning activities and measurable outcomes. Few faculty members have had formal education or training in instructional design or learning theory. To expect them to master the instructional design needed to put a well-designed course online in a relatively short period of development time is probably unrealistic (Oblinger & Hawkins, 2006).

But higher education is entering a difficult period financially, because a grow-ing number of states face declining tax revenues and budget deficits. According to Levine and Sun (2002), it will be difficult to sustain existing facilities, people, and programs to support distance learning initiatives. This will continue to have an impact on the resources to support faculty members in developing online courses. Another issue affecting the development of quality online courses is the lack of formal policies and procedures to ensure that online courses and programs are compliant with accessibility mandates. The 2010 data from the *Managing Online Education* survey (Green, 2010) reveal that 34 percent of the campuses participat-ing in the survey report that ADA compliance for online courses and programs resides with the individual faculty members who teach an online course, whereas 24 percent report that ADA compliance responsibilities resides with academic programs or departments. The 2010 survey also reported available instructional design resources and services to develop quality online courses were declining.

At the same time, higher education institutions face increasing demands from internal and external constituencies to engage in meaningful quality assurance to demonstrate the value and impact of their distance education efforts. The expectations for quality assurance of online courses are even higher in view of its relatively recent development and the rapid growth of learner interest. Two initiatives to address the issue of quality are outcomes-based curriculum and the Quality Matters program. The Spellings Commission (US Department of Education, 2006) report on the future of higher education was charged with recommending a national strategy for reforming postsecondary education, with a particular focus on how well colleges and universities are preparing learners for the twenty-first-century workplace. In the 2006 report, the commission focused on the standards of quality in instruction and accountability of higher education institutions in the ability to demonstrate learning outcomes. Learning outcomes of online courses have been scrutinized even more than traditional face-to-face courses. There has also been an outcry from industry and professional organizations that students are not prepared for the workforce and they have to spend additional resources to train new graduates as employees. An outcomes-based curriculum can help institutions achieve greater transparency and accountability for learner outcomes and provide a systematic process to ensure that outcomes are linked to competencies and demonstrable assessments.

The professional development of faculty is critical for the transition of courses from face-to-face to online because there are significant differences from the traditional to online environment (Cyrs, 1997). There is a need for *A Guide to Online Course Design: Strategies for Student Success*, which provides a guide to design quality online courses that meet specific standards for distance education courses. This need is driven by diminishing resources and increasing demands from internal and external constituencies to engage in meaningful quality assurance to demonstrate the value and impact of their distance education efforts.

AUDIENCE

The intended audience for this book comprises faculty members who are developing online courses. Instructional designers will also find this book valuable in focusing their efforts on quality standards and learning outcomes. Any institution delivering distance learning programs or individual online courses including colleges, universities, training departments, and other professional development centers for faculty members within higher education will find this book beneficial.

In addition, there are a growing number of virtual high schools who are training faculty members to develop online courses as well as people in governmental agencies and training departments within corporations who could find these materials valuable.

This book contributes to the body of knowledge on effective online course design by focusing on an understanding of who online learners are, how they learn, and what they have to overcome to achieve their educational goals online. The instructional strategies that we recommend in the book are grounded in instructional design theories and focus on specific strategies to help learners overcome challenges in learning and persisting in the online environment.

ORGANIZATION OF BOOK

In part 1, "An Introduction to Persistence and Quality Design," we introduce you to online learning, help you understand important persistence factors that affect learner success, and describe the design approach we will be taking in the book to help you design your online course. In chapter 1, "Quality Design to Support Learner Persistence," we discuss the need for online learning and define key persistence variables that affect online learners. We also consider quality standards for online course design to support learner persistence. In chapter 2, "The Instructional Design Process," we introduce you to a backward design approach that is based on an outcomes approach to course design. We also introduce you to the process you will use to design and develop your online course.

Using the foundations of persistence and quality design for online courses, part 2, "Analysis of Learners and Learning Outcomes," begins the design process with a front-end analysis of your learners and intended outcomes of your course. In chapter 3, "Analysis of Online Learner Characteristics and Needs," we look at the key attributes and needs of online learners and discuss how you can integrate this analysis into key design decisions for your online course. In chapter 4, "Analysis of Learning Outcomes and Competencies," we provide steps to help you through the process of an outcomes-based design of your course using a backward design process. The process includes brainstorming course outcomes and writing outcome and competency statements that describe the intended outcomes of your course.

Part 3, "Design of Course Assessments and Sequence," is the beginning of the design phase of the development process. In this part, you align assessments to your learning outcomes and determine a sequence of instruction. In chapter 5, "Design of Course Assessments," we show you the benefits of designing your assessments upfront to ensure proper alignment between your learning outcomes and the opportunities for your learners to demonstrate progress toward and achievement of outcomes and competencies. In chapter 6, "Sequence of Instruction," you determine the starting point for your instruction and create a sequence of instruction that aligns to the course learning outcomes and associated competencies.

Part 4, "Design of Instructional Strategies," is a continuation of the design phase in which you design instructional strategies to help learners achieve the intended outcomes of your course. In chapter 7, "Foundations of Transformative Learning," we discuss important learning principles and instructional strategies to ensure your learners are actively engaged in authentic course activities to support deep learning. We discuss active learning and how cognitive learning styles affect learning. We also discuss cognitive scaffolding strategies to ensure your learners are able to complete learning activities and achieve course outcomes. In chapter 8, "Selection of Instructional Materials," we discuss how to choose appropriate course materials that align with your course learning outcomes. We look at different types of text-based and media-based materials that can help learners understand key concepts and skills and provide strategies for locating and evaluating course materials to support your course design. In chapter 9, "Design of Effective Course Activities," we lead you through the process of designing instructional activities to support your learning outcomes and provide various examples that may be used in your online course to help learners turn the information they have gained through the instructional materials into knowledge. We also look at activities that provide authentic learning experiences and enable rich engagement, critical thinking, and problem solving.

Part 5, "Development of Instruction," moves you into the development phase of the course design process in which you will organize your content into units of study and then build it out in a web environment using a systems such as a learning management system (LMS). In chapter 10, "Development of Instructional Materials," we provide recommendations for how to structure units of study within your course and include a discussion of workload balance to ensure course activities and assessments are distributed reasonably throughout your course. We also help you develop an introduction to your course and discuss strategies to help clarify and communicate your expectations for learner participation throughout your course and ideas for helping learners acclimate to the online environment. In chapter 11, "Organizing the Course Environment," we look at how to build your course into the web environment you will be using, such as an LMS. We discuss important navigation and interface design considerations to ensure learners are able to easily locate and access course materials and activities and participate within your online course. We also discuss various tools and technologies you may implement to support interaction and facilitate presence in your online course.

Part 6, "Implementation and Evaluation," introduces the last phases of the development process. Because the book is focused on course design, we do not discuss implementation strategies. However, we discuss how to evaluate your course prior to implementation to ensure it meets quality standards for online courses. Chapter 12, "Course Evaluations and Maintenance," is the final chapter in the book and the only chapter in part 5. In this chapter, we help you conduct a final review of your course. We also discuss data collection post-implementation for the purpose of continuous quality improvement and finish up with a discussion of how to maintain your course over time.

We have created an online course design guide to accompany the text. This guide includes all of the steps discussed in the book to create your online course along with worksheets to help you think through each of the steps of the process. To access the online course design guide, go to www.josseybass.com/go /stavredes_herder.

About the Authors

Tina Stavredes has more than fifteen years of experience in online learning. Currently, she is Chief Academic Officer of Online Services at Corinthian Colleges, Inc. Prior to that, she spent ten years with Capella University serving in a number of roles, including director of curriculum, associate dean, chair, and as a Harold Able Distinguished faculty. Her experience includes managing and maintaining high-performing online faculty members and developing quality online courses. Prior to joining Capella, Dr. Stavredes worked as manager of academic technology support for the University of Minnesota's College of Education and Human Development.

Dr. Stavredes has a master's degree in education with a specialization in curriculum and instruction using information systems and technology in teaching and learning. Her PhD is in educational psychology with a specialization in cognition and learning as it relates to computer-based learning. She has been involved with online education and has demonstrated a passion and vision for how to build a quality and sustainable educational experience for online learners. Dr. Stavredes has an in-depth understanding of online learning communities, as well as communities of practice, from her experience teaching online and understands the pedagogy involved in building learning communities that are relevant and sustainable for the learner. She has also worked specifically with first-year online learners to understand the factors that lead to learner readiness and that affect persistence and retention. In her administrative roles, she has developed innovative ways to support quality teaching and help faculty members bring their expertise to the online classroom.

Tiffany Herder has worked in online learning for more than a decade. She has an MS in instructional design for online learning and works as a curriculum and instructional specialist, collaborating with faculty members and crossfunctional staff to create quality learning experiences. Ms. Herder also works as an online learning consultant helping to shape the direction of online learning and creating faculty and student development resources for institutions of higher education.

She has experience applying the Quality Matters program criteria to develop quality online courses. She also has worked extensively with faculty members developing and delivering workshops and just-in-time resources to support distance learning initiatives. Ms. Herder also has an expertise in outcomes-based curriculum development and translating curriculum requirements into high-quality and engaging online courses as well as developing authentic assessments to provide opportunities for learners to demonstrate outcomes. Finally, she continues to work to translate difficult concepts and create engaging learning experiences through the use of interactive multimedia and diverse instructional strategies.

An Introduction to Persistence and Quality Design

In part 1, we introduce you to online learning, help you understand important persistence factors that affect learner success, and describe the design approach we take in this book to help you design your online course. In chapter 1, "Quality Design to Support Learner Persistence," we discuss the need for online learning and define key persistence variables that affect online learners. We also consider quality standards for online course design to support learner persistence. In chapter 2, "The Instructional Design Process," we introduce you to a backward design process that is based on an outcomes approach to course design.

Quality Design to Support Learner Persistence

OBJECTIVES

After reviewing this chapter, you should be able to

- Analyze persistence models to identify challenges and barriers online learners must overcome to be successful in their programs of study to lay the foundation for effective course design.
- Analyze the role of course quality standards in course development to support the creation of effective online courses.

Online learning is at a crossroads. More and more individuals and institutions are turning to online learning as a way to meet a variety of learner, faculty, and administrative needs. According to the Sloan Consortium (2013), an organization dedicated to online education leadership, more than 6.7 million learners are taking at least one online course and 69.1 percent of higher education institutions state that online learning is critical to their long-term strategy. Financial pressures of dwindling enrollments, decreased funding, and high overhead costs are causing institutions to do more with less and look for alternative delivery methods for their curriculum. According to Allen and Seaman (2013), "online courses are those in which at least 80 percent of the course content is delivered online. Face-to-face instruction includes courses in which zero to 29 percent of the content is delivered online; this category includes both traditional and web-facilitated courses. The remaining alternative, blended (sometimes called *hybrid*) instruction has between 30 and 80 percent of the course content delivered online" (p. 7).

Institutions are offering a variety of instructional modes to meet the increasing demands from learners working full-time and needing flexible programs that meet their personal and professional goals.

With the rapid growth of online education, the focus has become the quality of learning outcomes from online courses. Reports show higher attrition rates for learners taking online courses so there is a growing need to understand factors that contribute to learner persistence in an online environment. The focus of this book is on the design of online courses that support learners' ability to persist in the online environment. Throughout the book, we refer to important concepts and strategies to support learner persistence. We also look at quality standards to support the design of an online course. In this beginning chapter, we present information on different persistence models that are relevant to online learning and help you understand important factors that may affect a learner's ability to successfully complete the course. We also discuss research on quality standards for online learning to help you create a quality online course that supports learners in achieving the intended learning outcomes.

DEFINING PERSISTENCE

Retention and *persistence* are sometimes used interchangeably, but they are not the same. *Retention* is the ability of the institution to retain learners from matriculation through graduation. *Persistence* is learners' ability to persist in their educational journey to degree completion. Learners can persist but may not necessarily be retained by the institution. For example, learners may decide they are interested in a different program of study offered at another institution or they may decide that they are not a fit with the institution and decide to change schools. They are actually persisting because they are continuing their education, but the institution's retention numbers decrease as a result of learners transferring. Therefore, focusing on persistence can help us better understand the factors that contribute to a learner completing a course or dropping out. Research shows that when learners complete a course, they are more likely to persist in the next course (Billings, 1988), so focusing on learners' completion course by course can set them up for additional success throughout their program. Persistence models help us identify critical learner needs and integrate effective teaching and learning strategies to support learners' continued success.

PERSISTENCE MODELS

There is a long history of research and conceptual models to explain learner behavior and perceptions related to persistence. Among these models are several that focus on the design of online courses and support online learner persistence — Billings (1988), Kember (1995), and Rovai (2003).

Billings Persistence Model

Billings's (1988) model focused on correspondence courses; however, there are a couple of important insights that helped drive some key design elements in the effectiveness of today's online courses. First, Billings talked about how learners who submit assignments early on in a correspondence course often persist longer than those who wait a couple of months to submit their assignments. This demonstrated that structured activity deadlines in a course, especially early on, would help learners continue to persist. He also correlated persistence with higher entrance examination scores, higher GPA, and higher courses completed with greater chances of persistence. Therefore, the more successes learners have, the more likely they will continue to be successful. This makes a case for designing an online course experience that provides a high level of support to help learners successfully complete the course. Additionally, Billings discusses the importance of learners' intentions to complete as a variable in persistence. He believes that learners can overcome other factors that may lead them to drop out if their motivation to complete is strong. This indicates a strong need to build motivational elements into an online course to help learners develop and sustain their momentum.

Kember Persistence Model

Kember's (1995) model focuses on adult learners in an open learning model of distance education. This model provides a nice linear path for learners in a course. The model starts with how learners' entry behavior and early experiences lead them down one of two paths—a positive path or negative path. A positive path leads to social integration and academic integration in which learners adopt a deep approach to learning and the goal is not simply to complete the course or get a good grade but to gain knowledge and tap into motivations related to self-improvement and enrichment. A negative path leads to a focus on excuses for their performance based on external issues such as insufficient time, distractions, or unexpected events that get in the way. This path results in a surface approach to learning in which the focus is not on gaining important knowledge that will have a positive impact on their lives but on simply completing the course. Motivation is based on external rewards rather than the joy or benefits of learning. This indicates the importance of setting up early experiences for encouragement and creating a support system inside and outside the course as well as the need to connect coursework to activities relevant to learners' personal and professional goals.

Rovai Persistence Model

Although the Billings and Kember models provide us with some important insights into persistence and course design, Rovai's (2003) model provides us with a comprehensive look at the variables that affect learners' persistence in an online learning environment. Rovai evaluated several persistence models relevant to nontraditional and online learners and developed a composite model to explain persistence of learners enrolled in online courses (exhibit 1.1).

Rovai integrates Tinto's (1975) student integration model and Bean and Metzner's (1985) learner attrition model, in particular, which are both grounded in early psychological models on persistence and the idea of learner-institution fit as a key indicator of persistence. He builds off of Tinto's and Bean and Metzner's learner characteristics prior to admission, such as age, ethnicity, gender, intellectual development, academic performance, and academic preparation, and adds skills learners need to develop to successfully navigate the online environment including computer literacy, information literacy, time management, reading and writing skills, and online interaction skills. In course design, these are elements that you can use as a basis to build in personalization and scaffolding to help learners achieve the learning outcomes regardless of their starting point.

Once learners are admitted to a program of study, there are additional factors external and internal to the institution that can affect learners' ability to persist. Rovai (2003) includes Bean and Metzner's external factors such as issues

Exhibit 1.1   Rovai Composite Persistence Model

Rovai Composite Persistence Model (Rovai, 2003)	Variables prior to admission	Learner characteristics: • Age, ethnicity, gender • Intellectual development • Academic performance • Academic preparation Learner skills: • Computer literacy • Information literacy • Time management • Reading, writing skills • Online communication skills
	Variables after admission	External factors (Bean & Metzner, 1985): • Finances • Hours of employment • Family responsibilities • Outside encouragement • Opportunity to transfer • Life crises
		Internal factors: • Tinto (1975): Academic integration, social integration, goal commitment, institutional commitment, learning community • Bean and Metzner (1985): Study habits, advising, absenteeism, course availability, program fit, GPA, utility, stress, satisfaction, commitment • Workman and Stenard (1996): Learner needs: clarity of programs, self-esteem, identification with school, interpersonal relationships, accessibility to support and services • Kerka and Grow (1996, as cited in Rovai, 2003): Learning and teaching styles

with finances, hours of employment, family responsibilities, the presence of outside encouragement, opportunity to transfer, and life crises such as sickness, divorce, and job loss. He also cites internal factors affecting learners after admission including variables researched by Tinto (1975), Bean and Metzner (1985), Workman and Stenard (1996), and Kerka and Grow (1996, as cited in Rovai, 2003). According to Tinto (1975), social and academic integration as well as goal commitment, institutional commitment, and the development of a learning community are internal institutional factors that affect persistence. According to Bean and Metzner, these internal factors include study habits, advising, absenteeism, course availability, program fit, current GPA, utility of the course, stress, satisfaction, and commitment. Rovai (2003) then added the work of Workman and Stenard (1996), who also analyzed learners' needs that influence persistence, and include consistency and clarity of online programs, policies, and procedures; learners' sense of self-esteem; ability to identify with the institution and not be looked at as "outsiders"; the need to develop interpersonal relationships with peers, instructors, and staff; and the ability to access academic support and services. Finally, the model shows that online learners expect their learning experiences to match their learning style, so attention to the use of a variety of instructional strategies is important to meet the individual learning styles of learners.

You may not be able to address all of these variables within the course design, but you can at least address the institutional factors such as helping learners feel like a part of the institution and directing them to the appropriate support resources. You can also help learners develop strategies to cope with external factors that require good time management strategies and ways to build a support network with their family and friends to support their learning. Finally, you can build relevant and engaging courses that help learners integrate into the learning community and build skills and knowledge relevant to their personal and professional goals. We discuss strategies to integrate these elements and the other persistence variables throughout the book.

QUALITY ONLINE COURSE STANDARDS

Because the quality of online learning has been debated in the field for some time now, there have been many efforts to define what elements go into a quality online course. More and more institutions are turning to quality programs and rubrics to ensure consistency among their online offerings. The difference between the practices we present in this book compared to these quality rubrics, however, is the focus on the design decisions. Most quality standards focus on learner satisfaction as a measure for what defines a quality course. In this book, we have focused on specific elements of the course design that contribute to greater learner persistence. A review of these standards can further support the design, especially if your institution subscribes to a specific quality rubric.

There are many different rubrics for evaluating the quality of online instruction. Many of the rubrics were created by individual universities or initiatives related to developing instructor knowledge and skills for designing effective online learning. The Illinois Online Network (1998–2006) is a faculty development initiative that provides professional development for online teaching and learning. They created a "Quality Online Course Initiative Rubric and Checklist" that focuses on seven categories — instructional design, communication, interaction and collaboration, learner evaluation and assessment, learner support and resources, web design, and course evaluation. California State University, Chico (2003), also developed a rubric with categories for learner support and resources, online organization and design, instructional design and delivery, assessment and evaluation of student learning, innovative teaching with technology, and instructor use of learner feedback to help define what a high-quality online course looks like. The Monterey Institute for Technology and Education (2010), an educational nonprofit organization, created the "Online Course Evaluation Project" to help assess and compare online courses and focuses on course developer and distribution models, scope and scholarship, user interface, course features and media values, assessments and support materials, communication tools and interaction, technology requirements and interoperability, and developer comments.

Currently, the most well-known rubric is the Quality Matters' rubric. The Quality Matters program is a "faculty-centered, peer-review process designed to certify the quality of online and blended courses." Funded by the US Department of Education Fund for the Improvement of Postsecondary Education, Quality Matters has become a leader in ensuring the quality of online education and received national recognition for its approach and improvement of online education and student learning (Quality Matters, 2011). Their rubric is based on extensive research in online learning and is composed of eight general standards and forty-one specific standards and includes annotations that provide examples of the application of the standards and the relationships among criteria. The eight standards include course overview and introduction, learning objectives (competencies), assessment and measurement, instructional materials, learner interaction and engagement, course technology, learner support, and accessibility (Quality Matters, 2011–2013).

As you can see from these few examples, although there are multiple rubrics available, the themes related to best practices and effective design for online learning are clear. Throughout the book, we integrate many best practices related to effective online learning design and supporting learner persistence based on the research on persistence and quality standards. Exhibit 1.2 describes these quality standards that are addressed in the book. Then, in chapter 12, you will do a final review of your course using a checklist of the criteria listed in the exhibit.

Exhibit 1.2 Quality Standards for an Online Course

Course Introduction

- The course follows university standards (insert specific standards in this review guide).
- On entering the course for the first time, learners can easily locate information to help them understand what to do (i.e., a "start here first" document).
- If the course is not based on a standard university template, you have provided a course orientation to the various course components and their function.
- There is an introduction to the course in the syllabus or faculty expectation statement describing the intended course outcomes.
- There is an introduction to how the course is structured in the syllabus or the faculty expectation statement (how long units are, weekly activities, deadlines). This may also be included in a course orientation if you have developed one.
- There are clear expectations for learners in a syllabus or faculty expectation statement (including required days in the course per week, expectations for discussions, absences from course, policies including plagiarism, code of conduct, and netiquette rules, due dates, and extensions).
- There is specific information about the minimum technical requirements for the course including hardware, software, and preferred browser.
- It also includes the minimum technical skills needed to participate fully in the course (i.e., ability to create and save files, attach documents, etc.).
- The instructor clearly communicates expectations regarding how to communicate with him or her as well as turnaround time for returning learner calls, e-mails, and so on. There are also descriptions of expectations for when discussions and assignments will be graded and returned to learners.

Course Outcomes, Competencies, and Objectives

- Course outcomes and competencies are clearly stated in a format that communicates the relevance of each outcome to the real world.
- Learning objectives clearly align to course outcomes and competencies.
- Learning activities clearly align to course outcomes and objectives.
- The prerequisite skills required for the course are clearly stated and are reasonable and appropriate to the learner population.

Instructional Resources and Materials

- All instructional resources and materials map back to the stated program outcomes and competencies.
- Clear instructions help learners understand how the instructional resources support the achievement of specific competencies and objectives.
- The instructional materials are written at a level understandable to the learner population.
- All instructional resources and materials have all required copyright clearance.
- All instructional materials are accessible to all learners following ADA standards such as screen readability and alternative presentation of materials.
- Multimedia elements are relevant to the course outcomes and competencies.
- Multimedia elements engage learners in the subject matter.
- The course effectively engages learners in the use of online resources.

Instructional Strategies

- Instructional strategies promote critical thinking.
- Instructional strategies promote improvement of writing skills.
- Instructional strategies are relevant to real-world application.
- Clear instructions include an explanation of how course activities fit within the structure of the course and its intended outcomes.

Exhibit 1.2 *(continued)*

Assessment and Feedback

- Course assessments are relevant to real-world application.
- Assessments clearly align to course competencies.
- Scoring guide criteria clearly align to course competencies.
- Assessment strategies provide appropriate opportunity for learners to demonstrate content knowledge and skills.

Course Introduction

- Assessment strategies provide appropriate opportunity for learners to demonstrate performance standards.
- Learners have opportunity for relevant practice prior to assessment of competencies.
- The course adequately prepares learners for practice activities.
- Learners have opportunity for formative evaluation prior to final assessment of competencies.
- The course adequately prepares learners for final learning outcome assessments.
- The course provides opportunities for instructor and peer feedback in a timely and consistent manner.

Presence

- The course provides opportunities to develop social presence.
- The course provides opportunities to develop instructor presence.
- The course provides opportunities to develop cognitive presence.

Course Structure

- The course structure is well organized with clear and logical flow from one topic to the next.
- The course presentation is consistent throughout units. For each unit of study, there is consistency in the layout of course materials and activities, including consistency in the nomenclature for headings and other elements of the course.

Clear Instructions

- Instructions are clear and concise.
- Instruction is formatted for easy on-screen reading.
- Instruction includes templates, worksheets, and examples to support learner success.

Course Workload

- The course contains an appropriate amount of coursework for the level of the course (complete course workload map to determine this criterion).
- The course workload is consistent throughout the course (complete course workload map to determine this criterion).

Use of Technology

- The course uses delivery methods appropriate to the learning activities.
- Learners have a clear understanding of the technology used in the course and how to use it.

Learner Support and Resources

- The course provides links to appropriate academic support resources (e.g., library, writing center) to enhance the learning experience.
- The course includes information regarding learner support services to resolve administrative and technical issues.

> ## Action Steps
>
> To help you apply the concepts in this chapter, complete the following:
>
> - Think about the reasons you are pursuing online learning and the pressures at your institution. Consider what you would like to accomplish as you dive into designing an online course.
> - Review the persistence models and the variables identified and note your initial reactions. Consider the following questions:
>   - Are there particular variables that seem to resonate with the experiences you've had with your learners?
>   - Are there particular variables that don't seem applicable to your particular population of learners at this time?

The Instructional Design Process

OBJECTIVES

After reviewing this chapter, you should be able to

- Evaluate backward design framework focused on creating aligned courses relevant to learners' professional and personal goals to lay the foundation for course design.
- Evaluate course development phases that create a structure for the design process for your online course.

Now that you have a foundational understanding of the outcomes for your online course, it's time to review how you get there. In this chapter, we discuss a framework of outcomes-based curriculum design and the phases of course development. This helps you gain a broader perspective of the process the book is structured on to help you achieve the end goal of a high-quality course built to support learner success.

With the focus on learning outcomes becoming more and more critical, we need a process that helps us design our online courses based on the key elements needed to help learners achieve learning outcomes. Outcomes-based curriculum design provides a framework to help align course content, activities, interactions, and assessments to build a cohesive, effective course focused on learner achievement.

Often, course design begins with the selection of a textbook and proceeds with dividing chapters into units, using discussion questions from the end of each chapter, and perhaps integrating the quizzes and other supplemental resources that come bundled with the text. Other times, instructional strategies are selected based on the individual faculty member's experience taking courses or on trial and error of what has worked in the past. This latter strategy is most often used when instructors do not have previous experience as online learners.

BACKWARD DESIGN FRAMEWORK

Grant Wiggins and Jay McTighe (2005) have created a backward design framework called Understanding by Design that focuses on engaging learners in exploring and deepening their understanding of important ideas. The design method begins at the end, with the desired result, or learning outcomes, then moves on to identify the evidence needed to demonstrate achievement of the learning outcomes, and, finally, the instruction to guide learners to the desired results. It is called backward design, or assessment-first design, because it is the opposite of a more traditional course design approach in which content drives the development of units and instruction and assessments are created at the end of the process. In their text, Wiggins and McTighe (2005) outline three stages: identify desired results, determine acceptable evidence, and plan instruction and learning experience (figure 2.1)

Stage 1 of the planning process answers the question, "What should learners be able to do as a result of the instruction?" This critical question helps you determine the knowledge, skills, and attitudes that are most important for learners to demonstrate, and at what level they should be able to perform them by the end of the course. During this stage, you develop learning outcomes to identify priorities for course instruction that guide the design of appropriate assessments and instructional strategies. In stage 2, you answer the questions, "How will I know if learners have achieved the desired results and have met the overall outcomes for the course?" and "What will I accept as evidence of learner understanding and proficiency?" This is when you move to design and develop assessments that enable learners to demonstrate learning outcomes as

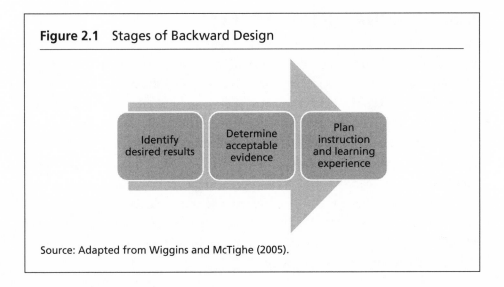

Figure 2.1   Stages of Backward Design

Identify desired results

Determine acceptable evidence

Plan instruction and learning experience

Source: Adapted from Wiggins and McTighe (2005).

well as opportunities to check for understanding, determine progress, and identify difficulties and misunderstandings along the way. Finally, in stage 3, you plan the instructional content and learning experiences to support the achievement of course outcomes. Wiggins and McTighe (2005) recommend the following questions to be considered during this stage:

- What enabling knowledge (facts, concepts, and principles) and skills (procedures) will learners need to perform effectively and achieve desired results?
- What activities will equip learners with the needed knowledge and skills?
- What will need to be taught and coached and how should it best be taught, in light of performance goals?
- What materials and resources are best suited to accomplish these goals? (pp. 18–19).

Throughout the book, we will use this backward design framework to ensure your course design focuses on outcomes and everything you design aligns specifically with the course outcomes. We position this backward design framework, however, within a larger structure of instructional design that includes analysis at the front end and evaluation and continuous improvement at the back end.

INSTRUCTIONAL DESIGN PROCESS

Although the backward design model provides a core framework to ensure that assessments and instructional activities are aligned with course learning outcomes, additional steps are necessary to ensure that the course helps support learner persistence. The field of instructional design provides numerous models for how to design a course. For the purpose of this book, we have chosen not to dive into these models because our focus is not to teach you how to be an instructional designer, but to help you successfully design a course for the online environment. Instead, we will focus on a simple, instructional development process—analyze, design, develop, implement, and evaluate. Many individuals refer to this process as *ADDIE*. The following sections outline the major phases of ADDIE and the process we take you through in this book to design an online course that supports learner persistence.

Analyze

During the analyze phase, you will get to know your learners better by understanding their key characteristics and needs. You will also determine the purpose of the course within the curriculum. Key questions you will address include the following:

- Who are your learners and what are their characteristics?
- What are your learners' key needs to support their persistence?
- What is the purpose of the course within the broader curriculum?

Design

Once you have conducted a front-end analysis of the learner population, you will engage in design activities that create the core elements of the course. This includes creating learning outcomes that serve as the foundation for the course and aligning assessments and instructional strategies within an appropriate structure and sequence to enable learner achievement of the course learning outcomes. You will also analyze and balance the workload associated with course activities to ensure a consistent experience for learners. Key questions you will address include the following:

- What knowledge, skills, and attitudes will learners gain from completing the course?

- What opportunities will you provide to enable learners to demonstrate progress toward and achievement of learning outcomes?

- What is the appropriate sequence and structure to support learners' achievement of the learning outcomes?

- What course materials and multimedia will help learners develop the knowledge, skills, and attitudes necessary to demonstrate the learning outcomes?

- What activities will enable learners' successful demonstration of competence in the assessments?

Develop

During the develop phase, you will craft the instruction for your assessments and course activities as well as additional context information such as unit objectives, introductions, and a syllabus. You will also develop scaffolding to support learners so they can successfully complete course activities and demonstrate achievement of the learning outcomes. Finally, you will build your online course in your online tools or learning management system (LMS). Key questions you will address include the following:

- How will you clearly communicate your expectations for learners' performance and participation in course activities?

- What support tools and scaffolding are necessary to enable learners' performance given their previous knowledge, skills, and attitudes?

- How will you create a simple and effective interface and layout to enable learners to easily navigate and complete course activities within the online course environment?

Implement

The implement phase of course development occurs when you launch your course and use a variety of strategies to facilitate the online course. Because this book is focused on course design, we do not include implementation and facilitation strategies. For an in-depth look at effective teaching strategies for online courses, see Stavredes's 2011 book *Effective Online Teaching: Foundations and Strategies for Student Success.*

Evaluate

In the final phase, evaluate, you will conduct a final evaluation of your online course and consider strategies for continually evaluating the course after implementation. Key questions you will address include the following:

- How well are learners performing on the learning outcomes?
- What does learners' performance on assessments and activities tell you about the effectiveness of the course design?
- What barriers and challenges are learners running into throughout the course?
- What improvements could you make to improve learner persistence and successful achievement of course learning outcomes?

As you can see from the questions in the evaluate stage, the course development phases are a cycle. Once you get to evaluate, you may start again to improve the outcomes of the course. As we take you through this process, we will use a visual display to help you orient yourself to the steps you have completed, where you are now, and what is left in the process.

Figure 2.2 is an example of the figure of the design process we will use throughout the book. The inner circle represents the stages of the development process: analyze, design, develop, and implement and evaluate. For each step there are several decisions you will need to make, which are represented in the rectangles. In the introduction for each of the parts, we will include the design process figure to help orient you to what's ahead. The upcoming steps in the process will be called out with a larger pie piece and description for the activities you will participate in. In this example, you are about to begin the develop phase where you will develop instruction and develop web navigation and interface.

In addition, we have created an online course design guide to accompany the text. This guide includes all of the steps we discuss in the book to create your online course along with worksheets to help you think through each of the steps of the

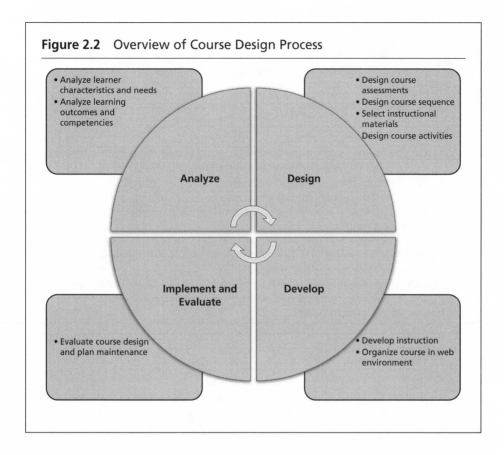

Figure 2.2 Overview of Course Design Process

- Analyze learner characteristics and needs
- Analyze learning outcomes and competencies

- Design course assessments
- Design course sequence
- Select instructional materials
- Design course activities

Analyze

Design

Implement and Evaluate

Develop

- Evaluate course design and plan maintenance

- Develop instruction
- Organize course in web environment

process. To access the online course design guide, go to www.josseybass.com/go/stavredes_herder.

In this chapter, we discussed the course design process that we use throughout the rest of the book. You will go through the process of analyzing, designing, developing, and evaluating in upcoming chapters. You will also use a backward design approach to ensure your entire course focuses on your intended learning outcomes. We also incorporate important quality standards and elements to support persistence throughout the design process. Next, we begin the course development process by completing an audience and needs analysis to understand important characteristics and needs that learners will have entering the course.

Action Steps

To help you apply the concepts in this chapter, complete the following:

- To make sure you are focusing your online learning within the constraints and resources of your institution, connect with your administration to see what resources are currently available, including quality rubrics. Consider using the following questions:
  - Do you provide any support resources such as training or instructional design staff to support the development of my online course?
  - Are there learning management systems or online tools that are supported by IT that I could use?
  - Do you offer any other resources or tools to help me make the shift to online learning?
  - Do you offer any financial incentives for creating online courses?
  - Do I need to review any quality standards or rubrics to ensure my course is appropriate for the institution?
- Reflect on your current approach to course design and consider the shifts you must make to your approach to align with an outcomes-based and backward design approach.

Analysis of Learners and Learning Outcomes

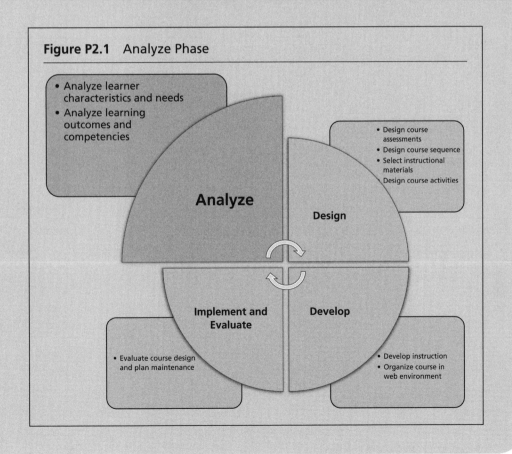

Figure P2.1   Analyze Phase

- Analyze learner characteristics and needs
- Analyze learning outcomes and competencies

Analyze

Design

- Design course assessments
- Design course sequence
- Select instructional materials
- Design course activities

Implement and Evaluate

Develop

- Evaluate course design and plan maintenance

- Develop instruction
- Organize course in web environment

Using the foundation of learner analysis from the previous chapters, part 2 begins the design process with a front-end analysis of your learners and intended outcomes of your course. In chapter 3, "Analysis of Online Learner Characteristics and Needs," we look at the key attributes and needs of online learners and discuss how you can integrate this analysis into key design decisions for your online course. In chapter 4, "Analysis of Learning Outcomes and Competencies," we walk you through the process of an outcomes-based design of your course using a backward design process. The process includes brainstorming and drafting course outcomes and competency statements that describe what you expect learners to achieve by the end of your course.

3

Analysis of Online Learner Characteristics and Needs

OBJECTIVES

After reviewing this chapter, you should be able to

- Analyze key characteristics of online learners that will affect their ability to achieve the intended learning outcomes of the course.
- Analyze the needs of your online learners that should be considered and integrated into the design of the course to support persistence.

You could say that the basic purpose of education is change — increasing knowledge, changing behavior, shifting perspectives, adding skills, and much more. Focusing on the variables related to persistence helps support change in learners. Unless they continue through their educational experiences to completion, learners will not achieve the outcomes we set forth for them and the personal and professional goals they set for themselves.

Effective learning and course quality begins with an understanding of your learners. In the traditional instructional design model, this phase is called analyze. In the beginning of this phase, you figure out the needs, potential persistence problems, and key characteristics of your audience — your learners. This chapter is focused on techniques to reflect on the characteristics, skills, and needs of your learners.

ONLINE LEARNER CHARACTERISTICS

According to data from Noel-Levitz's (2012) *National Online Learners Priorities Report*, the majority of online learners in the United States are

- Caucasian females enrolled full-time
- Undergraduates employed full-time
- Married home owners
- Planning to complete degrees online
- Taking fewer than six credits
- New to online programs

Forty-five percent of learners also have a goal of completing a master's or doctorate degree. Although these characteristics represent the current majority of online learners in the United States, online learners are a heterogeneous and diverse population from a variety of cultural and educational backgrounds.

One commonality among this population, however, is the main reason learners engage in online learning—flexibility. Online learning enables learners to pursue their educational goals while balancing a number of roles and responsibilities in their lives. Even four-year schools are seeing more learners working more than twenty hours a week and supporting dependent children (Public Agenda, 2010, as cited in Picciano, Seaman, & Allen, 2010). The reduced logistical demands, increased flexibility, enhanced technology, and reduced opportunity cost of online learning is becoming appealing to more and more learners (Dzuiban, 2009, as cited in Picciano, Seaman, & Allen, 2010). As the number of learners who take online courses continues to increase, it is critical to understand how to support learners to overcome challenges and be able to engage, persist, and successfully achieve their goals.

LEARNER PERSISTENCE

In chapter 1, we discussed Rovai's composite persistence model that is relevant to online learners. First, let's consider what Rovai calls *learner characteristics:* this includes Tinto's (1975) initial attributes as well as Bean and Metzner's (1985)

Exhibit 3.1   Key Questions for Identifying Important Learner Characteristics

Learner Characteristics	Key Questions
Age, ethnicity, gender	• What demographic information is available for your institution regarding age, ethnicity, and gender? • Does your course follow your institution's trends or does the course include a different division of age, ethnicity, and gender?
Residence status	• Is there a residential option at your institution? • What is the breakdown of onsite versus offsite learners? • What segment does the course trend toward?
Educational goals	• What are learners' reasons for pursuing an education? • Why did learners choose your institution? • Does your institution focus on specific career goals? • Do you see a wide range of those goals in the course or are learners focused on similar educational goals? What are they? • To what level of education do learners aspire (bachelor's, master's, doctoral, etc.)? • How important is completing a degree to your learners? • What are the trends of your learners in completing at your institution? Do they typically transfer?
Academic performance (prior GPA)	• How successful were your learners in their previous educational experiences? • How successful were they at your institution prior to your course?
Academic preparation (precollege schooling)	• What types of experiences might your learners have had prior to enrolling at your institution? • What types of experiences might they have had prior to your course?

background and defining variables. Exhibit 3.1 outlines some key questions to consider for each of these learner characteristic variables.

Taking the time to answer these important questions can help you understand your learner population in order to design your course to meet the needs of your learners.

Minimum Skills Necessary to Complete an Online Course

Another important aspect to consider is the skills learners need to be successful in an online learning environment. Rovai (2003) outlines five key areas of skills learners need to be successful: computer literacy, information literacy, time management, reading and writing, and computer-based interaction. In today's wired world, we often assume a certain level of technical competence and comfort with using computers and online tools. However, learners choosing online courses may vary in their knowledge, abilities, and comfort with technology. This variability makes it very important to gauge your learners' skill levels so you can design these aspects into the course, as necessary. Information literacy skills are also important in an online environment. Many learners compose their discussions and assignments based on information they find online without a thought about the validity and reliability of the information. Many online learners will not even attempt to use your institution's online library for peer-reviewed information because of the difficulty they face when trying to use it. Additionally, because learners can complete their coursework anytime, it often turns into "no time" and they begin to quickly fall behind. Online learners need to have good time management skills. Often, the online environment is extensively made up of reading assignments and composing written responses to discussions and written assignments, so learners with poor reading and writing skills may have difficulties in an online environment. Finally, because all interaction is via the computer, learners who are more social and verbal in a face-to-face environment may have difficulty. If learners are not comfortable with or cannot use the technology required for the course or do not have the prerequisite time management, information literacy, computer-based communication, and reading and writing skills, it doesn't matter how well you design the learning experiences. The technology and entry skills themselves will be barriers to learner persistence.

There has been much study of learner readiness for online learning given the evidence that dropout rates among distance learners are higher than those of traditional, campus-based learners (Allen & Seaman, 2010). One way to think about your learners' skills is to create a rubric based on your own course. For computer literacy, information literacy, time management, reading and writing, and computer-based interaction, create a list of the minimum skills necessary to complete the course. Exhibit 3.2 provides an example you can use as a starting point to consider the types of skills learners need.

Exhibit 3.2 Minimum Skills Necessary to Complete an Online Course

Skills	Low (What skills do learners need to come into the course with that could not be learned during the term?)	Average (What does the average learner need to be able to do to be successful in your course?)	High (What skills might advanced learners come into the course with?)
Computer literacy	Turn on a computer, access an online course, and use word processing software	Turn on a computer, access an online course, use attachments, and use word processing software	Turn on a computer, access an online course, use attachments, use word processing, database, spreadsheets, and visual media software, and troubleshoot online access and other computer issues
Information literacy	Use a search engine (e.g., Google)	Access online libraries and databases but may not be able to locate high-quality articles; locate resources online using a search engine to support learning	Use online libraries and databases to locate high-quality resources and articles
Time management	Able to adhere to deadlines	Able to adhere to deadlines and is self-motivated	Able to adhere to deadlines, is self-motivated, able to break tasks into component parts and complete throughout a unit or module
Reading and writing	Read and write at a grade school level	Read and write at a high school level	Read and write at a college level
Computer-based interaction	Able to post to discussion boards	Able to post to discussion boards and effectively interact with individuals via electronic means	Familiar with social media and able to post to discussion boards and effectively interact with individuals via electronic means; able to personalize communication

Another approach is to look at the readiness instruments available for under-standing if a learner is ready for online learning. Dray, Lowenthal, Miszkiewics, Ruiz-Primo, and Marczynski (2011) completed a review of readiness surveys and found that many online programs have a survey of some kind to help learners determine whether or not they should pursue an online course. It may be helpful to search for a readiness tool online. You can do a search of "Are you ready for online learning?" or simply "online learning readiness" to find these tools. You may choose to adopt or adapt one of these instruments to use yourself or simply use the questions with your learners to ensure you have communicated with them the skills they will need to be successful in your course.

Environmental (External) Factors

Next, let's take a look at what Bean and Metzner (1985) label as "environmental variables" and what Rovai (2003) labels as "external factors" in exhibit 3.3. These are elements that are external to the academic institution and your course, but, nonetheless, affect learner persistence. As you think through these questions, you will most likely come up with multiple answers to address the variety of learners at your institution and in your course.

Exhibit 3.3 Environment Variables (External Factors) Affecting Persistence

External Factors	Key Questions
Finances	• Do learners have a financial plan in place for their education prior to your course? • Are they able to afford courses or are they constantly struggling to keep up with financial demands? • Will their financial aid be dispersed early enough so they can purchase their books?
Hours of employment	• What does your institution's data say about the number of hours learners tend to work while going to school? • How many hours do your learners tend to work? • Do you have learners who are working full-time?
Family responsibilities	• What does your institution's data say about the number of learners who are married or have children? • What are the trends in your course?
Outside encouragement	• Do learners have support from outside the institution and your course such as family, friends, and colleagues?
Opportunity to transfer	• Do learners at your institution typically tend to transfer to another institution to complete their study? • If so, do they see the courses offered and your course as helping them transfer to another institution?
Life crises	• What types of life crises might affect your learners given the answers to your previous questions, for example, sickness, divorce, or job loss?

Often, you can infer the answers to these questions based on your previous experience with your learners either face-to-face or online. If you are creating a new course, you may need to make some educated guesses based on your institution's data. If you are new to online learning, you may also want to connect with other instructors who have taught online at your institution. The online version of your course may target a different set of learners than your face-to-face course. Consider the information regarding characteristics of online learners at the beginning of the chapter to help you think through these questions.

At this point, you may be thinking that spending the time to go through these questions and look at these factors is excessive — that it would take you hours to answer all of these in detail. However, the point of these questions is to become more aware of the factors that may affect your learners' ability to persist and try to make design decisions that better support learners in being able to overcome some of the variables. As you continue to work with your learners online, you will gather additional insights into their key characteristics and the reasons they drop or persist in your course, which can help you continually improve the quality of your course.

Once you have a better understanding of your audience, the next step is to translate these learner attributes into needs that will help you determine the key elements to address in the design of your course.

LEARNER NEEDS

It's important to understand the needs of your learners by conducting a needs analysis to help you think about the elements necessary for learner success in your course. Many of these needs come from the audience analysis such as a need to learn how to navigate an online course or use word processing software based on your learners' technological skills. Other needs may come from the persistence models we talked about such as a need for program clarity to ensure that requirements are easy to understand so learners can complete their programs efficiently. We will take another look at your audience analysis in this section as well as revisit the key learner needs outlined by persistence models.

First, let's revisit learner characteristics. Depending on the diversity of learner characteristics, you may see consistency or variety in your learners' needs. These can range from connecting your learning activities to specific career motivations to designing specific support to help your learners fill gaps in their preparation for your course. Exhibit 3.4 provides a way to think through the key needs of your online learners. You may also have additional ideas based on your previous experiences with your learners and your audience analysis.

Again, don't become overwhelmed thinking you have to incorporate each of these considerations into the design of the course, but have a clear understanding of the needs, so your design reflects and supports your learners. Throughout the book, we provide you with specific strategies to support your learners and help them persist.

Exhibit 3.4   Online Learner Needs

Learner Characteristics	Example of Key Needs
Age, ethnicity, gender	• Awareness of cultural needs and issues • Awareness of gender-based communication differences • Interpersonal relationships with others • A range of special needs depending on learners' lives, for example, families or marriage
Residence status	Depending on your learners' residence status, they may need • Few to no hours necessary for onsite activities (especially part-time and offsite learners) • Communication that helps them feel like a part of the institution • Instructor presence and support • To feel like a part of a learning community
Educational goals	• Connections to their motivational influences • Course activities connected to their educational goals • Job enhancement or personal enrichment opportunities • Clear program and course requirements • Courses to fit within their schedule • Programs and courses to fit their goals • A satisfying course experience
Academic performance (prior GPA)	• If learners have low prior GPAs and poor experiences with education—small wins to prove to themselves that they can be successful • If learners have high prior GPAs—confirmation that they can do well in your course
Academic preparation (precollege schooling)	• Opportunities to get support for skills they are lacking such as effective study habits or time management • Clear contact information and accessibility to advising and other learner support services
External Factors	
Finances	• Clear contact information and accessibility to financial services • Reinforcement of the benefits to their education despite financial uncertainty

Exhibit 3.4 *(continued)*

Learner Characteristics	Example of Key Needs
Hours of employment	• Clear deadlines and strategies for balancing work and course activities • Stress-management strategies • Support to build effective study habits
Family responsibilities	• Clear deadlines and strategies for balancing work and course activities • Reinforcement of the benefits to their education despite current stress
Outside encouragement	• Strategies to build a network of family and friends to support their education • Opportunities to build relationships with instructors and learners for support for their education
Opportunity to transfer	• Reinforcement of the benefits of education and ability to transfer credits from courses to another institution to complete, if necessary • Transparent connections between coursework and future job prospects
Life crises	• Strategies for dealing with stress • Flexibility to complete course activities during life crises

With your audience and needs analysis in hand, in chapter 4, we consider curricular analysis to help you determine the goals for your course and how those connect to some of the audience characteristics and needs you determined for your learner population.

Action Steps

To help you apply the concepts in this chapter, complete the following:

• To work through these questions for your own learner population, use the exhibits in this chapter to consider your learners' key characteristics and needs.
• Review the data available to you from your institution's internal and external websites related to your learners. If necessary, connect with the department in charge of data at your institution and ask for any additional insights regarding your learners' demographics and behavior.
• Connect with instructors who have taught online previously at your institution or a related institution nearby. Ask them some of the questions related to learners and their needs to gather additional insights about your potential online learners.

Analysis of Learning Outcomes and Competencies

OBJECTIVES

After reviewing this chapter, you should be able to

- Analyze the purpose of a course within a curriculum framework to determine appropriate course learning outcomes.
- Use taxonomies of learning to define types of outcomes and performance expectations for the course.
- Brainstorm skills, knowledge, and attitudes to develop an understanding of the intended outcomes of the course.
- Construct effective learning outcome statements that communicate to learners the outcomes and competencies they will achieve at the end of the course.

The Spellings Commission on the Future of Higher Education (US Department of Education, 2006) was charged with recommending a national strategy for reforming postsecondary education, with a particular focus on how well colleges and universities are preparing learners for the twenty-first century workplace. In the 2006 report, the commission focused on the standards of quality in instruction and accountability of higher education institutions to demonstrate learning outcomes of learners. At the same time, there has been an outcry from industry and professional organizations that learners are not prepared for entry into the workforce, which requires additional resources in terms of time and money to train new graduates as employees. This has resulted in a new curriculum design that focuses on outcomes and associated competencies that situate learning in the context of authentic learning experiences that prepare learners for the workplace.

Focusing on learning outcomes in the design of a course helps provide a systematic way to ensure the course supports the achievement of skills, knowledge, and attitudes needed in the real world. Creating outcomes for the course that are achievable given your learners' previous academic preparation and performance can help learners persist because the content and activities support greater learner success. Developing course outcomes that help learners establish a knowledge and fact base necessary for application of key concepts as well as providing opportunities to connect learning with previous knowledge and practice skills all help create a foundation for a quality course.

LEARNING OUTCOMES DEFINED

The Council for Higher Education Accreditation (2001) defines learning outcomes as "the knowledge, skills, and abilities that a learner has attained at the end (or as a result of) his or her engagement in a particular set of higher education experiences" (p. 14). Learning outcomes may be written at the program level to describe what learners will attain at the end of a program or written at the course level to indicate what learners will attain at the end of a course.

Learning outcomes help learners understand the specific skills, knowledge, and attitudes they will gain from a course. When worded clearly and accurately, outcomes also provide important information regarding expectations for learners' performance. This helps learners develop a greater understanding of what they can expect from a course, which can improve motivation and engagement. Learning outcomes also help the institution communicate the value learners receive from their experience and set expectations for the course experience. Finally, learning outcomes help guide the design of learning experiences within a course or program by aligning course activities, materials, and assessments to learning outcomes.

CURRICULUM ANALYSIS

In a top-down approach to curriculum development, courses are organized around a common set of outcomes that make up a program of study. At the course level, specific learning outcomes directly align to the overall outcomes for the program of study. If your institution practices this type of approach to curriculum development, learning outcomes may exist for the program or programs of study related to your course. Even if your program does not have formal learning outcomes, the program owner or faculty leadership often has a vision and understanding of the overall goals of the curriculum. To determine the purpose of your course within the context of the curriculum, consider the following questions:

- What are the overall outcomes for the program of study your course is a part of?
- What professions and roles does the program of study prepare learners for?
- How do those outcomes relate to learners' fields of practice and future professions?
- What external standards, if any, do the program outcomes align with?
- When do learners take your course in the program sequence?
- What are the prerequisites for this course? What skills, knowledge, and attitudes do those courses address?
- Is this course a prerequisite for any other course(s)?
- Are there any core general learning skills that need to be addressed in the course (for example, critical thinking and information literacy)?
- Are those core skills delivered in other courses throughout the curriculum?
- What else do I need to know about the program and specialization context of this course?

If you cannot answer these questions, consult someone from the program leadership to make sure you have a complete understanding of how your course fits within the program of study before you begin developing the course.

To illustrate the importance of understanding where your course fits in the overall curriculum of a program of study, let's go through a quick example with an English writing course. Exhibit 4.1 provides example responses to the key questions.

In this example, the course is part of the general education curriculum that is a part of all associate and bachelor programs. In other cases, you may find that the course you are designing is one of the core or elective courses in a specific program such as psychology, accounting, or information technology, so your answers will be more specific to how the course fits within the curriculum and

Exhibit 4.1 Curriculum Analysis Example

Key Questions	Responses
What professions and roles does the program of study prepare learners for?	Various—course relates to developing effective communication skills across all programs and specializations
What are the overall outcomes for the program of study your course is a part of?	• Communicate effectively • Critical thinking • Information literacy
How do those outcomes relate to learners' fields of practice and future professions?	Wide range of applications in learners' fields including paper publications, business communication, presentations, grant writing, and more
What external standards, if any, do the program outcomes align with?	Effective communication in writing is integrated into many professional organizations and specialization accreditation standards
When do learners take your course in the program sequence?	During the first year of their program
What are the prerequisites for this course? What skills, knowledge, and attitudes do those courses address?	Technically, no prerequisites; learners come in with a wide range of previous writing, critical thinking, and research skills
Is this course a prerequisite for any other course(s)?	Technically, no, but course provides foundational writing skills for future courses
Are there any core general learning skills that need to be addressed in the course (for example, critical thinking, information literacy, etc.)?	This is a general education course, so it aligns directly to the general education outcomes.
Are those core skills delivered in other courses throughout the curriculum?	Yes; all courses in the general education curriculum include these core skills.
Are there any other elements to consider related to the program and specialization context?	Many instructors note that learners come into their programs and courses with poor communication skills and problems ranging from grammar and mechanics to writing paragraphs to using the writing process. They feel that if we can improve the writing course, they will be able to focus more attention on advanced competencies within their courses.

the field. In those cases, you will have many more parameters within which you will need to align your course.

Once you have an understanding of how your course fits with the overall curriculum, you will be able to make connections within the course to the rest of the curriculum. Next, you will need to think about how to translate this context to specific learning outcomes for the course and connect these outcomes to learners' educational goals.

TAXONOMIES OF LEARNING

You will develop a set of learning outcomes that describe what your learners will have learned and at what level by the end of the course. To help further define learning outcomes, competencies are used to articulate the major skills, knowledge, and attitudes that help learners achieve the course learning outcomes. Competence means being able to perform in context, so each competency statement should include qualifying conditions of performance in which the competency will be demonstrated. Figure 4.1 illustrates the breakdown of knowledge, skills, and attitudes. Knowledge helps learners develop a strong information base

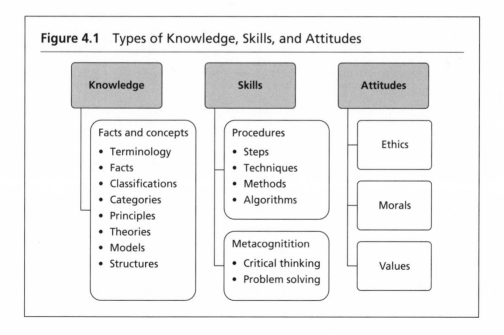

Figure 4.1 Types of Knowledge, Skills, and Attitudes

including facts, concepts, and important terminology from the field of study, classifications and categories of facts, as well as principles, theories, models, and structures. Skills help learners develop procedural knowledge such as steps, techniques, methods, and algorithms used in the field of practice. It also includes metacognitive skills to support critical thinking and problem solving. Attitudes help learners understand how to act using ethics, morals, and values in the professional field.

One of the most widely used frameworks for organizing levels of complexity in learning is Bloom's taxonomy (Bloom, Englehart, Furst, Hill, & Krathwohl, 1956). There are three taxonomies based on three domains of learning:

- *Cognitive (knowledge):* "The recall or recognition of knowledge and the development of intellectual abilities and skills"
- *Affective (attitudes):* "Changes in interest, attitudes, and values, and the appreciations and adequate adjustment"
- *Psychomotor (physical skills):* "The manipulative or motor-skill area" (pp. 7–8)

The cognitive domain is the most widely applicable across courses and has been recently updated to account for recent advances in education and learning theory (Anderson & Krathwohl, 2001). The framework is broken down into six levels:

- Remember
- Understand
- Apply
- Analyze
- Evaluate
- Create

The taxonomy is hierarchical with each level being subsumed by the higher levels. For example, a learner at the application level has already mastered the content at the knowledge and comprehension levels. The framework also lays out four types of knowledge: factual, conceptual, procedural, and metacognitive (learning about learning). Although there are other frameworks that may be useful in classifying learning outcomes, Bloom's taxonomy is the most widely used and accessible across programs and fields.

Knowledge

Knowledge, both factual and conceptual, is simply the information that learners need to remember and it is considered the lowest level of Bloom's taxonomy of knowledge and comprehension. It is critical that learners have a well-developed knowledge base, so your outcomes should ensure that learners understand the meaning of terminology and have a basic comprehension of classifications, categories, principles, theories, models, and structures necessary to apply those concepts if they do not already have those coming into the course. However, knowledge is not enough in the real world. Learners also need to be able to use the knowledge in order to solve problems and perform in real-world settings. Putting facts into practice helps learners gain the skills to transform factual and conceptual knowledge into procedural knowledge. Teaching learners how to use knowledge in context helps ensure long-term retention and the ability to transfer knowledge to performance in professional settings.

Skills

Skills are part of procedural knowledge and answer the question of when, where, and how to use declarative knowledge. Skills are usually associated with the psychomotor domain of Bloom's taxonomy, which includes physical movement, coordination, and the use of motor skills. Often, however, looking at skills in a broader sense can support additional course outcomes. Skills can include the psychomotor domain, if relevant, but also include mental skills such as critical thinking and problem solving, which help learners develop an understanding of when, where, and how to use certain facts and employ specific procedures to solve problems.

When confronted with a problem, learners need to be able to access their knowledge base, determine relevant information, and develop a strategy to solve the problem. This type of knowledge is metacognitive and requires the ability to organize the factual, conceptual, and procedural knowledge learners have accessed, interpret incoming information, and develop an appropriate strategy.

As you can see from this definition of the skill competency, it uses the higher levels of Bloom's taxonomy, which leads to deep learning.

Attitudes

Attitudes relate to the affective domain of Bloom's taxonomy and include emotions, feelings, values, and appreciation, to name a few. This type of outcome often relates to ethics in the field or valuing different knowledge and skills as they relate to practice.

Bloom's Taxonomy Verbs

Bloom's taxonomy helps in the development of competencies in a couple of ways. First, it helps to further analyze the level of understanding you want your learners to accomplish with your course. For instance, are you teaching an introductory course? Do learners need to learn basic concepts and simple application? In that case, learning outcomes may be at the lower levels of Bloom's such as *understand* and *apply*. Or is your course more advanced and learners need to evaluate experts' works or create original works? In that case, the higher level skills *evaluating* or *creating* are more appropriate.

Second, the taxonomy helps you select language that clearly illustrates your expectations. For each level in Bloom's taxonomy, verbs have been selected to help guide you in defining outcomes such as *create, analyze, apply*, and *differentiate*. Exhibit 4.2 provides an illustration of the different levels of Bloom's taxonomy and popular words used for each level. As you develop your outcome statements, consider the different action verbs to describe the highest level of understanding that you expect learners to achieve by the end of the course.

COURSE ANALYSIS

The first step in developing learning outcomes for your course is to brainstorm the skills, knowledge, and attitudes you want learners to achieve. In many instances, you probably have a good idea of what you want learners to get out of your course even if you haven't created specific learning outcomes in the past. Reflect on the following questions:

- What do you want learners to take with them from this course?
- What are the core skills, knowledge, and attitudes related to the purpose of the course?

Exhibit 4.2 Verbs Associated with Bloom's Taxonomy

Remember	List, define, tell, identify, show, label, collect, examine, tabulate, quote, name, who, when, where
Understand	Summarize, describe, interpret, contrast, predict, associate, estimate, discuss, extend
Apply	Apply, demonstrate, calculate, complete, illustrate, show, solve, modify, relate, change, experiment, discover
Analyze	Analyze, separate, order, connect, classify, arrange, divide, compare, select, infer, distinguish, differentiate
Evaluate	Assess, decide, rank, grade, test, measure, recommend, convince, select, judge, discriminate, support, conclude, compare, justify
Create	Combine, integrate, modify, rearrange, plan, create, design, invent, compose, formulate, prepare, rewrite, construct, produce

- How are those skills, knowledge, and attitudes related to the learners' educational goals and profession?

- What is the purpose of building those skills, developing that knowledge, or taking on those attitudes?

- What is the context in which learners would use the skills, knowledge, and attitudes?

You may also want to consult external associations and professional organizations related to the discipline or subject matter, if applicable. Often, these associations have standards of practice for professionals in the field that can help you align the course learning outcomes to professional standards of practice. Job searches and a literature review about key competencies for the field can be helpful as well. This work is often done at a program level, but can also be helpful to ensure that course learning outcomes are relevant to your learners. If this work was completed at the program level, reviewing the professional standards that the outcomes align to can help you further clarify the purpose of the course.

Free Writing

Once you have thought about these questions and completed some preliminary research, free writing can be a helpful strategy to get your major ideas in a written form. Try to imagine your learners a year, five years, or ten years from now and think about the critical learning you would want them to have and how they could apply what they've learned in the course to their lives at that time — personally and professionally. The idea is to get as many ideas down as you can without making corrections or judging your results. Here is an example of free writing from our English course example:

> Writing and communication skills are foundational to learners' career and personal life no matter what program of study they choose. They will need to be able to communicate personal and professional thoughts and ideas in a way that is clear, concise, and legible. This includes creating effective presentations, writing effective papers, as well as the development of professional day-to-day communications such as e-mails, office memos, and other documents.
>
> Learners will be able to communicate their ideas in these forms clearly, succinctly, and effectively using proper writing conventions. They will know how to adapt their communication styles for different stakeholders such as peers, management, and leadership. Learners will also need to carefully construct quality compositions, which requires time and several drafts. The writing process can be used to brainstorm the purpose of their communication, outline key ideas, annotate research, when appropriate, and draft and revise compositions. Learners will also be able to craft logical thoughts and arguments using critical thinking. This includes the ability to locate relevant research and use evidence to support the information they present in their compositions.

As you can see from the example, the focus is on what learners can do with a strong focus on real-world applications. Free writing will help you identify major skills for your outcomes as well as help you start to think about the purpose of your outcomes and how to communicate that purpose to your learners.

Visual Concept Map

A visual concept map is another useful tool for brainstorming that helps you organize your thinking visually. If you have Microsoft Office, you may have the drawing tool Visio or you can simply use Word's drawing tools to create a canvas and insert shapes and text. In addition, there are a number of free concept-mapping tools on the web, or you can use the simplest of tools, a pen and piece of paper, to visualize major concepts, skills, and attitudes. To start, put your course at the middle and then use bubbles to represent the competencies you think are important to the course. Draw lines between items that are connected. A digital application can be better for this work because you can move items around depending on the relationships you determine as you start mapping. If you are using pen and paper you can cut your paper into pieces or use sticky notes and write ideas on a single piece of paper, which will enable you to easily move them around and organize them. Figure 4.2 provides an example of a concept map for the English course example.

Now, review your brainstorming activities. Are there any skills, knowledge, and attitudes that are used in practice together? Are there any elements that build off of one another? If so, group those together. These will be used to develop the different learning outcomes for your course. If not, you may want to go back to your exercise and see how you think the different elements you brainstormed could fit into a cohesive course. You may have thought of too many disparate elements you want to achieve or may have brainstormed what learners should achieve at the end of multiple courses. You may need to start prioritizing the knowledge, skills, and attitudes now or at least start thinking about how you could connect the different parts. If necessary, go back to your curricular analysis to review how the course fits with the other courses in the curriculum. Also, think about which knowledge, skills, and attitudes are essential to the purpose of the course or are just nice for learners to know to start prioritizing your ideas, as necessary.

LEARNING OUTCOME STATEMENTS

When writing learning outcome statements, it is important to use verbs that describe exactly what learners will be able to do on completion of your course. There are some verbs that are unclear in the context of an expected learning outcome statement such as *know, be aware of, appreciate, learn, understand, comprehend*, or *become familiar with*. These words and phrases are often vague, have multiple interpretations, or are simply difficult to observe or measure (American Association of Law Libraries, 2005). It is best to avoid using these terms when creating learning outcome statements. For example, consider the following learning outcomes statements:

> The learners will *understand* basic personality theory.
> The learners will *appreciate* individual differences.

Figure 4.2 Concept Map Example

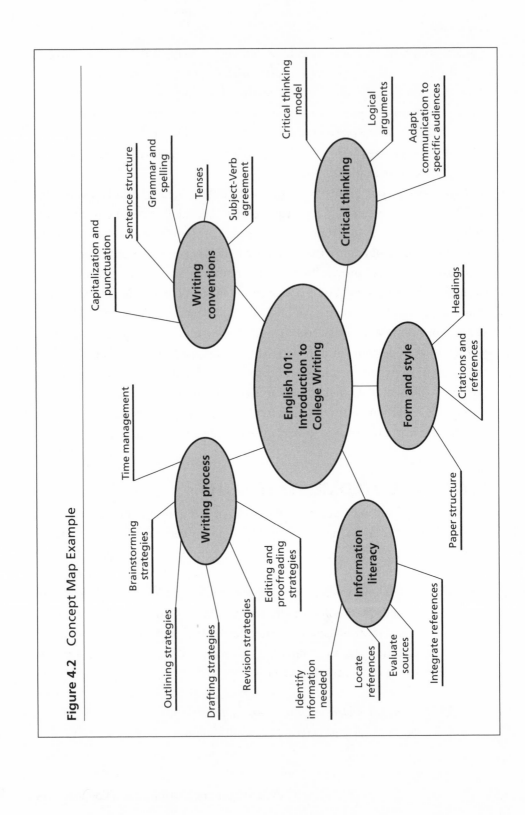

Both of these learning outcomes are stated in a manner that makes them difficult to assess. How do you observe someone "understanding" a theory or "appreciating" individual differences? How easy will it be to measure "understanding" or "appreciation"? Instead, focus on crafting learning outcomes that are simple, direct, and clear statements that learners can easily grasp. By reviewing exhibit 4.2 you can ensure that the verbs you use produce statements that can be assessed. To ensure this clarity, Quality Matters (2011–2013) recommends avoiding educational jargon, confusing terms, unnecessarily complex language, and puzzling syntax (the order in which words appear).

Now, you are ready to construct learning outcome statements that communicate to learners what they can expect to learn as a result of taking the course. The best place to start is with the actual skills, knowledge, or attitudes you listed in your brainstorm. Then, you can add the purpose or reason it's important to attain the competency. Finally, you can add a specific, active verb to the beginning to create your statement. Exhibit 4.3 breaks down the components of an outcome statement with an example for an English course. This will help you break down the knowledge, skills, and attitudes that make up your learning outcomes and help you develop outcome statements.

With the components of your outcomes and a bit of revision to smooth out the wording, the learning outcomes become as follows:

- Apply the writing process to create effective writing products such as papers and presentations.

Exhibit 4.3 Components of Outcome Statements

Active Verb	Skills, Knowledge, Attitudes	Purpose	Real-World or Field or Educational Goal Connection (external standards, if applicable)
Apply	Writing process	Create effective writing products (papers, presentations, etc.)	Grant writing, presentations, publications, e-mails, and business communication
Adhere	Writing conventions	Effectively communicate ideas	All communications
Adhere	Form and style	Clearly and concisely present ideas	Publications, properly differentiate between own and others' ideas
Integrate	Critical thinking	Provide logical and adequate support for ideas	Persuade others to make a decision

- Adhere to conventions of standard written English to effectively communicate ideas.

- Apply appropriate form and style to clearly and concisely present ideas.

- Integrate critical thinking strategies to provide logical arguments and adequate support for ideas to persuade the target audience.

The number of learning outcomes for the course will vary depending on the credits for the course but, typically, should be no more than three to five to ensure adequate time for learners to achieve them. During the process of developing learning outcomes, it is important to clarify and prioritize those outcomes to focus your learners on the most critical skills, knowledge, and attitudes. You may be inclined to include every detail learners would ever need to practice your subject matter in the field. As you draft your outcome statements, go back to your audience analysis and think about whether or not learners may achieve the learning outcomes you draft within the time frame of the course. Also, think about how your course fits into the curriculum. If the course is foundational, some of the more advanced knowledge, skills, and attitudes may be inappropriate for the course and may be developed later in the program. Likewise, if your course is more advanced, some of the more basic skills already may have been developed in the prerequisite courses.

COMPETENCY STATEMENTS

Once you determine your learning outcomes, next identify specific competencies for each outcome that will provide direction to how learners will achieve the stated learning outcomes. As you created your concept map, you were thinking about competencies needed in practice, so you already have a start on this step. Now, you can look back at your concept map and begin organizing the individual competencies that make up your outcomes. One way to think about breaking a learning outcome down into competencies is to think about what a learner must demonstrate. What must learners do to achieve the outcome? What must learners know? You may also think about a developmental path. What are the steps needed to take learners from the novice level at which they start the course to achieving the learning outcomes by the end of the course? The following is an example of how we further defined our learning outcomes for the English course in terms of competencies.

- Apply the writing process to create effective writing products such as papers and presentations.
  - Use brainstorming and outlining strategies to initiate the writing process.
  - Locate scholarly and practitioner resources appropriate to the audience and writing purposes.
  - Use drafting and revising strategies to refine the writing products (papers and presentations).
  - Proofread papers and presentations to correct grammar, mechanics, and usage issues.
- Adhere to conventions of standard written English to effectively communicate ideas.
  - Use appropriate capitalization and punctuation.
  - Use appropriate sentence structure.
  - Follow grammar rules including tenses and subject-verb agreement.
  - Spellcheck work and correct any misspellings.
- Apply appropriate form and style to clearly and concisely present ideas.
  - Use appropriate paper structure based on a relevant style guide.
  - Cite references appropriately in text and at the end of the paper in a reference list or bibliography according to the style guide.
  - Use appropriate headings.
- Integrate critical thinking strategies to provide logical arguments and adequate support for ideas to persuade the target audience.
  - Practice using a critical thinking model to evaluate and construct arguments.
  - Develop logical arguments using proper support.
  - Adapt communication to specific audiences.

CHECKLIST FOR OUTCOME STATEMENTS

Now, that you have developed your learning outcomes and associated competencies, let's review your outcome statements. Exhibit 4.4 lists questions for you to ask as you review your learning outcome statements. If you find yourself answering "no" to any one of the questions, revise your statements accordingly.

Let's look at some examples of outcome statements to see if they contain all of the components described and include the elements of being observable, measurable, and relevant to the real world:

- *Example 1:* Discuss theories of personality psychology.

- *Example 2:* Apply theories of personality psychology in an initial assessment of a new client.

- *Example 3:* Conduct an initial assessment of a new client using theories of personality psychology as the framework for your assessment.

In example 1, learners are asked to discuss theories of personality; however, the importance of understanding theories of personality in psychology is unclear. In example 2, it is clear that learners must be able to apply theories of personality to an initial assessment of a new client; however, the level of application may not be the highest level that is expected in the course. In example 3, it is clear that the theories are being used as a framework to conduct the initial assessment, so it communicates clearly to learners how theories of personality psychology are used in practice and it is stated at the highest level of the taxonomy expected in the course. As you can see, we continued to develop the outcome statement to state the highest level of attainment needed in practice. Crafting outcomes that fulfill the criteria of being observable, measurable, and relevant as well as being clear to learners and instructors may take some time. You may continue to refine your outcomes and competencies as you continue on with developing your course. At this point, it is important to have a clear direction and focus for your course learning outcomes so they are relevant to your learners' educational and professional goals.

Exhibit 4.4   Checklist for Outcome Statements

Key Questions	Revision Strategies
Are they worded as a learner-oriented, essential competence (psychomotor, cognitive, and affective) to be achieved by the end of the course?	Remove any references to what learners will do to achieve the outcomes such as reading articles, practicing processes, or writing papers. Envision experts in the field using these outcomes to further remove the competencies from the academic context and position them within real-world practice.
Are they at the highest level of performance expected for this course?	Review the most advanced or complex use of the knowledge, skills, and attitudes expected in the course and adapt the language to ensure the outcomes communicate that highest level. Use figure 4.1 to determine the level.
Are they worded in clear, specific, unadorned, and concise language readily understood by the learner and instructor?	Review them from the perspective of a learner or someone outside of your field. Define any jargon or field words learners may be unfamiliar with. Have a peer or learner review the outcomes and provide suggestions for revision.
Are they measurable, in other words, can you craft assessments that will evaluate learners' achievement of the outcomes?	Start to think about the types of assessment you may want to use to have learners demonstrate the outcomes. Start to think about evaluation criteria for their performances. Replace any fuzzy words such as *understand* or *demonstrate* that have many interpretations.
Are they action oriented and begin with the verb that most precisely describes the actual, preferred outcome behavior to be achieved?	Review Bloom's or other taxonomies with corresponding words, a thesaurus, or professional organizations' outcomes and content to brainstorm more precise words.
Are they consistent with standards, practice, and real-world expectations for performance?	Review external standards related to your outcome and information about learners' educational goals and future professions to align outcomes and competencies to the field practice. Review job descriptions for related positions to see what employers expect from successful candidates.
Do they contribute to the cluster of abilities needed by the learner to fulfill the expected overall performance outcomes of the field of practice?	Review program outcomes and related external standards and align outcomes and competencies to expectations.

In this chapter you developed an understanding of an outcomes-based approach to course design and reviewed the taxonomies of learning. You also participated in a brainstorming activity to determine learning outcomes for the online course you are designing and developed outcomes statements. Now that you have refined the learning outcomes and competencies for your course, we will determine appropriate assessments that demonstrate that learners have achieved the intended course outcomes. In chapter 5, we take an in-depth look at how to develop effective assessments.

Action Steps

To apply the concepts in this chapter, complete the following:

- Determine the purpose of your course within the context of the curriculum (exhibit 4.1). If you are unable to answer the questions yourself, consult with the leadership of the program for more information.
- Brainstorm the skills, knowledge, and attitudes you want learners to achieve during the course. Complete the free-writing activities and a concept map to document your brainstorm.
- Identify themes within your brainstorm to shape your main learning outcomes.
- Construct learning outcome statements to communicate to learners what they can expect to learn as a result of the course. Use exhibits 4.2 and 4.3 in the chapter to help form your statements.
- Evaluate your learning outcomes and competencies using exhibit 4.4 and refine your statements until you have a workable draft to use for brainstorming assessment strategies.

Design of Course Assessments and Sequence

Figure P3.1 Design Phase Part One

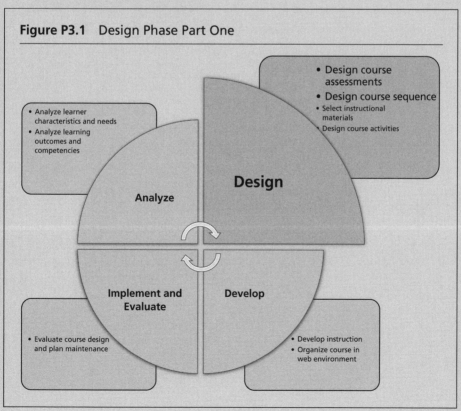

Part 3 is the beginning of the design phase. In this part, you align assessments to your learning outcomes and determine a sequence of instruction. In chapter 5, "Design of Course Assessments," we show you the benefits of designing your assessments up front to ensure proper alignment between your learning outcomes and the opportunities for your learners to demonstrate progress toward and achievement of outcomes and competencies. In chapter 6, "Sequence of Instruction," you determine the starting point for your instruction and create a sequence of instruction that aligns to the course learning outcomes and associated competencies.

5

Design of Course Assessments

OBJECTIVES

After reviewing this chapter, you should be able to

- Brainstorm appropriate types of assessments for your online course based on course learning outcomes and competencies.
- Integrate multiple assessment strategies to gather appropriate evidence of learners' achievement of course learning outcomes.
- Integrate formative assessment opportunities to provide feedback on learners' progress toward achieving course learning outcomes.

In chapter 4, you developed outcomes for your course and outlined associated competencies in terms of individual skills, knowledge, and attitudes necessary to achieve the learning outcomes. In this chapter, you will think about how to assess learners in order to be sure they have actually achieved the intended outcomes of the course. By developing assessments at the beginning of the course design process, you can ensure that later efforts of designing instructional strategies focus on the type of learning needed to demonstrate the achievement of the intended learning outcomes of the course.

PURPOSE OF ASSESSMENTS

In the design of a course, assessments have two major purposes: to provide learners an opportunity to demonstrate achievement of outcomes and to demonstrate progress toward the learning outcomes (figure 5.1). By providing learners an opportunity to reflect on their progress toward goals and receive feedback that helps them understand where they excel and areas they need to focus additional effort, they are able to build higher levels of competence. Gathering data from assessments can also help you determine how well your learners are performing in order to implement just-in-time strategies to improve learning. These two purposes translate into different types of assessments: summative and formative. Summative assessments enable learners to demonstrate the extent to which they have achieved the learning outcomes of the course. Formative assessments provide an opportunity for learners to demonstrate their development toward the learning outcomes and provide constructive feedback to learners about their progress to ensure they can achieve the intended outcomes by the end of the course. Often, individual outcomes in a course are integrated into one summative assessment in the form of a final project, paper, or exam. Other times, your outcomes may be distinct enough that you will have multiple summative assessments throughout the course.

Once you know what your final summative assessments are, you can determine where learners need formalized feedback to progress and can design appropriate formative assessments that provide the needed feedback. For your formative

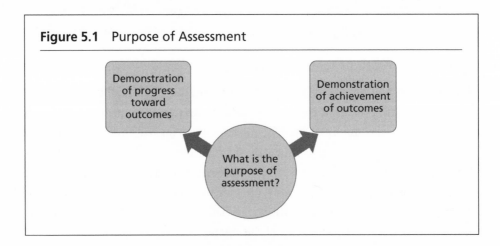

Figure 5.1 Purpose of Assessment

Demonstration of progress toward outcomes

Demonstration of achievement of outcomes

What is the purpose of assessment?

assessments, you may have learners submit subsections of a final project for review such as an audience analysis or annotated bibliography or you may have them participate in a short case study within a single unit before tackling a larger case study that spans several units of study and requires greater competence. You may also use formative assessments to assess learners' foundational knowledge prior to higher level application or analysis activities. For example, you may give learners a quiz to ensure they understand grammar and mechanics rules in writing before having them apply it by constructing a small paragraph or larger paper.

Using a range of formative and summative assessments in the course helps move your design away from high-stakes assessment. High-stakes assessment is the use of few assessments at the summative level designed to evaluate learners' demonstration of course outcomes. This is often done with a midterm exam covering the first half of the content and a final either covering the second half of the content or the full course. The concern about this assessment strategy is that it doesn't provide learners with an opportunity to receive feedback along the way. Without this feedback, learners may encounter many difficulties and misunderstandings in their coursework and will not be able to assess and correct those performance issues prior to a summative assessment.

Assessments should be designed as soon as you develop your learning outcomes. Designing assessments at this point provides a foundation for the design of instructional strategies to ensure you are choosing strategies that help learners achieve the course outcomes. It also helps you continue to refine the wording and focus of your outcomes. As you start to brainstorm how learners may demonstrate your outcomes, you will continue to think about how those outcomes are practiced in the field and how learners may practice them in the course.

TYPES OF ONLINE ASSESSMENTS

There are many types of assessment to consider for your online course. Exhibit 5.1 provides a summary of the various types of assessment including authentic assessment, test, self-assessment and reflective assessment, portfolio, and collaborative assessment.

Authentic, Performance-based Assessments

Often, outcomes-based courses focus on authentic, performance-based assessments. Authentic assessments focus on the application of knowledge, skills, and

Exhibit 5.1 Types of Online Assessments

Assessment Types	Description	Use	Examples
Authentic, performance-based assessments	Based on real-world application of knowledge, skills, and abilities; often incorporates problem solving and critical thinking skills	Performance skills, critical thinking, and problem solving	Creating a business presentation, writing a song, completing an experiment, or interviewing an expert
Self-assessments or reflective assessments	Encourages learners to reflect and write about their personal thoughts about course concepts	Attitudes, values, dispositions, or habits of mind	Journals, blogs, other reflective essays, or online learning-readiness assessment
Portfolios	A collection of documents representative of learners' work over time	Show learning and growth over time, showcase exemplar work, show process for completing a larger project, or highlight important artifacts from a program and career	Demo tape, compilation of marketing artifacts, papers, or an art portfolio
Collaborative and peer assessments	Focuses on the work of a team rather than an individual and includes learners' assessment of work by other learners	Team building and collaboration skills	Team creation of a marketing plan for a new product, managing an IT project as a team, or an original composition collaboration project
Tests	A more traditional form of assessment using multiple choice, matching, true-false, and short-answer questions	Knowledge, conceptual understanding, or application and analysis	Recalling music history eras, applying basic medical terms, or calculating opportunity costs

attitudes in practice and often incorporate problem solving, critical thinking, and other higher level skills. Examples of this type of assessment can range from business projects, compositions, experiments, problem-solving projects, case studies to a number of discipline-specific activities that assess learners' ability to apply what they've learned in real-world situations and applications.

Self-Assessments or Reflective Assessments

Self-assessment and reflective assessments encourage learners to reflect on their own personal thoughts about course concepts and write about them. According to Stephen Brookfield (1987), reflective learning is an important part of critical thinking. Reflection enables learners to consider where they have been, where they are, and where they want to go. With this knowledge, learners can grow as self-directed, independent learners who are in control of their own learning. Self-reflection enables learners to develop plans for continual improvement by helping them see areas of growth and areas that need additional attention to improve cognitive development and attain the intended outcomes of the course.

Reflection can be used to assess professional attitudes, values, dispositions, or personal habits of the mind. These assessments can also be paired with other assessments to help learners explain the process they went through during an authentic assessment. Self-assessments can also be used as a primer at the beginning of a course or activity to determine learners' previous knowledge and experience and where they need to focus their attention to achieve the learning outcomes by the end of the course. This use is especially helpful with learners who have previous experience with the subject matter.

Portfolios

A portfolio is a collection of documents that represent learners' work over time. It is another type of assessment that is becoming more popular as technology facilitates the gathering of artifacts. This type of assessment enables you to see the evolution of learners' work, showcase their best work throughout a course, or show the process for completing a larger project. It can also be a great way to assess learners' program outcomes in a final capstone course. Examples include a demo tape highlighting learners' original musical compositions, a compilation of marketing strategies for multiple projects, or an art portfolio that shows multiple works.

To develop this type of assessment, you will need to identify specific criteria for judging the learners' work. In addition, you will want to consider how you evaluate the progression of learners' work over time to see how the artifacts they submit in their portfolio demonstrate how they have deeper knowledge and understanding.

Collaborative and Peer Assessments

Collaborative and peer assessment focuses on the work of a team rather than an individual. This type of assessment is great for collaborative and team-building outcomes. Similar to authentic assessments, the examples are various and include the development of a team marketing plan for a new product, managing an IT project as a team, or an original composition collaboration project such as a song or work of art. One of the issues that learners have with teams is their grade is affected by other learners' performances; therefore, the total grade should not be based solely on a final team product. Learners should be able to earn a top grade for their contributions even if all of the members of the team are not fully engaged. Consider grading individual deliverables by team members rather than the project as a whole, so individual learners who have done their part will not be negatively affected by issues that may occur within the team. When grading the team, consider criteria that relate to what makes a good team member (Stavredes, 2011), including the following:

Team environment: Contributes to building a constructive team environment by participating in the team activities on a regular basis and contributing to team meetings

Integrity: Builds trust with team members by acting ethically and putting the team above his or her own individual contributions

Accountability: Follows through on agreed-on tasks and responsibilities as required by the project

By focusing on criteria that relate to being a good team member, learners can be satisfied that those learners who choose not to participate fully will not be able to earn the same grade as those that do, which can lead to greater satisfaction with team activities.

Tests

Finally, tests are a type of assessment that is commonly used in courses. This form of assessment is focused on knowledge, concepts, or application and analysis when there is a single answer. An important issue to consider when designing tests is the characteristics of online learning. In a face-to-face course, you have much more control over the assessment environment. You may have learners check their notes, textbooks, calculators, and phones at the door. You may also set aside a specific time for all learners to complete the assessment so everyone takes it at once and cannot share answers or questions with each other. In the online environment, you cannot completely control the test environment. Online, all assessments are open book because they are taken in learners' own environments where you cannot keep them from opening their books or reviewing other resources. Also, with tests in an electronic form, it becomes very easy for learners to share test questions. However, there are strategies to mitigate these concerns. You can use a timed test so it is difficult for learners to simply look up the answers in the allotted time. You could also generate a set of random questions that assess the same knowledge but with different questions. This enables you to generate a unique test for each learner and make it more difficult for learners to share test information.

Test Blueprints

You have more than likely developed tests in the past, but we thought we would share some strategies for aligning your tests to your learning outcomes. Suskie (2009) suggests using a test blueprint, or outline of your learning outcomes, to develop your test. A test blueprint can help you ensure that the most important outcomes are addressed and thinking skills are emphasized rather than trivia knowledge. It also can help ensure you have an adequate amount and quality of test questions to be able to demonstrate the achievement of outcomes.

At this point, you have already developed course learning outcomes. Next, you need to determine which outcomes you will assess with a test. You will need to consider the competencies associated with the outcomes and develop objectives that align to each competency. Similar to the relationship between competencies and learning outcomes, objectives indicate important points of demonstration of a competency. Here's an example of a start to a test blueprint based on one of the outcomes for the English writing course example:

Learning Outcome

Apply the writing process to create effective writing products such as papers and
  presentations.

Competency

Use brainstorming and outlining strategies to initiate the writing process.

Objectives

Articulate the purpose of brainstorming in the writing process.

Describe three methods for brainstorming ideas.

Articulate the purpose of outlining in the writing process.

Describe the main parts of a writing product.

Identify the appropriate method for organizing writing products.

Competency

Locate scholarly and practitioner resources appropriate to the audience and writing purpose.

Objectives

Articulate the purpose of resources in a writing product.

Identify information needed for a writing product.

Identify the appropriate database for locating information for a writing product.

Competency

Use drafting and revising strategies to refine writing products (papers and presentations).

Objectives

Articulate the purpose of drafting in the writing process.

Describe the differences among quoting, paraphrasing, and summarizing.

Describe key strategies for drafting a writing product.

Articulate the purpose of revising in the writing process.

Describe key considerations and issues to address in revisions.

Competency

Proofread papers and presentations to correct grammar, mechanics, and usage issues.

Objectives

Articulate the purpose of proofreading in the writing process.

Describe key considerations and issues to address in proofreading.

Describe strategies for proofreading writing products.

Articulate the difference between revising and proofreading.

Once you have the blueprint outlined, you can create the test questions that align to each of the items.

There are a number of excellent resources that provide a more in-depth discussion of how to design assessments. We recommend the following:

- Cohen, A., & Wollack, J. (n.d.). *Handbook on test development: Helpful tips for creating reliable and valid classroom tests.* The authors are from the University of Wisconsin and their online handbook outlines many best practices in developing tests.

- Palloff, R., & Pratt, K. (2009). *Assessing the online learner: Resources and strategies for faculty.* San Francisco: Jossey-Bass.

- Suskie, L. (2009). *Assessing student learning* (2nd ed.). San Francisco: Jossey-Bass.

CHOOSING FORMATIVE AND SUMMATIVE ASSESSMENTS

We have discussed several types of assessments you can use in your online course. The goal is to incorporate many different types of assessments in the course to assess the degree to which learners have met the intended outcomes of the course. This ensures that learners have adequate opportunities to demonstrate competency as well as opportunities for feedback at the foundational and conceptual levels as well as the application, analysis, and creation levels of understanding. The more opportunities you can provide learners to receive feedback along the way, the greater opportunity there is to develop deeper learning.

It also helps develop learner confidence and motivation. Often, learners become anxious about assessments and may have low motivation because they feel that they are not smart enough to demonstrate high performance. To develop learner confidence, provide early assessments at the lowest level of understanding in order to provide an opportunity for all learners to demonstrate some level of competence. This will help build their confidence and motivate them to engage in the course. It will also help ensure learners have adequate foundational knowledge before moving on to higher levels of performance. Then move on to higher levels of assessments as learners gain a solid foundation. Exhibit 5.2 provides suggestions for the different assessment strategies with ideas for how to use them as formative assessments and summative assessments.

ALIGNING ASSESSMENTS TO LEARNING OUTCOMES

Now that you have some foundational knowledge of the purpose of assessment and different types of assessment, let's move on to how to design assessments based on your learning outcomes. Consider the following steps as you develop your assessments:

1. Review your learning outcomes for the course and reflect on the following questions:
   - How will you know if learners have achieved the outcomes or goals?
   - What will you accept as evidence of understanding and proficiency?
   - How might learners use the outcome in the real world? What is a real-life task associated with the learning outcome? If there are no specific real-world tasks, what makes the outcome relevant to learners?
   - What are the relationships among your outcomes? Would any of them be performed, demonstrated, or used together?
   - At what level do you expect learners to demonstrate each outcome?
2. Review your answers along with exhibit 5.1 to determine the appropriate types of summative assessments. You may be able to integrate your outcomes into a single, final assessment or you may need to have multiple assessments to cover your range of outcomes. Be sure to set challenging but realistic expectations for your learners.

Exhibit 5.2   Formative and Summative Assessment Strategies

Assessment	Summative	Formative
Research paper	Final draft research paper	• Summary of research topic • Annotated reference list • Concept map of paper • Outline of paper • Research analysis worksheet • Assignments based on specific outcomes related to the research
Literary analysis paper	Analysis of large book	• Analysis of individual chapter • Short writings on different themes
Business proposal	Final business proposal	• Business idea • Problem statement, gap analysis, opportunity analysis • Market, competition, competitive edge, risks • Product description, marketing strategies, financial needs
Project	Final project	• Project plan or proposal • Individual components of project
Test	Final test that assesses deep understanding of knowledge	• Quiz that assesses basic foundational knowledge: multiple choice, T/F, match, fill in the blank, short essay
Case study	Large case study that requires integration of major course concepts	• Short case studies that assess individual concepts, for instance, The National Center for Case Study Teaching in Science: http://sciencecases.lib.buffalo.edu/cs /collection or Ethics in Mental Health Research: https://sites.google.com/a /narrativebioethics.com/emhr/contact
Graded discussion	No summative assessment; discussions should be used as a formative assessment and align to assignments	• Discuss individual concepts • Compare and contrast • Discuss cause and effect • Debate • Analyze • Role-play • Share news article related to course concept • Select a topic • Brainstorm
Self-assessment or reflective assessments	Course reflection; encourage learners to reflect and write about their personal thoughts about course concepts	• Journal entries • Blog • Project reflection • Assignment reflection
Portfolios	A collection of documents representative of learners' work during the course	• Individual components of the portfolio

3. Once you have an idea of how learners will demonstrate learning outcomes in a summative assessment, think about some of the key steps in the process for learners to get feedback along the way. Reflect on the following questions:

- Do any of the components of the assessment build on one another?

- Are there any components that are critical to the success of the other components?

- Are there any common misconceptions or frequent misunderstandings involved with any of the components?

- Is there a more simplified application of these skills, knowledge, or concepts that could be used as practice for a more complex application later?

- Is there any basic information or conceptual understanding learners need before they can move on to application of the skills?

- Are there any places for which feedback is absolutely essential?

- Are there any elements for which it would be good to know learners' previous knowledge, skills, and attitudes?

4. Use the answers to those questions to determine additional formative assessments needed in the course.

5. Capture key notes about your assessment to help guide the rest of your development.

Let's take a look at the English writing course example and walk through the process of brainstorming summative and formative assessment strategies. As you review the outcomes, it is clear that all of these outcomes are ideally integrated with communication in the field and may be integrated into a single summative assessment at the end of the course. Reviewing the information about the program and the purpose of the course, you will see many different authentic applications that may be relevant to different learners. To help ensure that the assessment strategies are relevant to learners, the course will be designed to enable learners to select from various authentic writing products such as a grant, research proposal, or business case presentation, or they may propose a final writing product of their own based on their professional interests and goals. Also, because the first outcome is about the writing process, learners will submit a portfolio of their work throughout the course including brainstorming ideas, outlines, annotated references, and several drafts.

To provide learners with adequate feedback throughout the process, however, there are multiple formative assessments needed for each outcome. Because the range of learners' skills are varied coming into the course, there will be self-assessments for each outcome to help learners understand where they need to focus additional effort. In addition, quizzes will be used to assess whether learners have developed the foundational knowledge and skills needed for the writing process, writing conventions, form and style, and critical thinking. An audience analysis will help learners think through the audience they are writing for. An annotated bibliography will be used to ensure learners are integrating appropriate references, analyzing the value of the resource and communicating that value clearly in writing, using correct form and style to ensure they are able to cite their sources properly, and thinking critically as they evaluate their resources. Once they have constructed an annotated bibliography, learners will complete an "argument analysis worksheet" to further assess their critical thinking to ensure they understand multiple perspectives on an issue and can distinguish specific arguments and evidence authors to support their position. An outline and draft will also be submitted for peer and tutor review to provide additional feedback prior to the final assessment. Exhibit 5.3 provides an example of assessment strategies for an English writing course and how they relate to the outcomes.

By thinking through the questions we've provided, you will be able to align your assessments to your outcomes and understand exactly what evidence you will need to determine the extent to which learners have achieved the outcome. From there you can determine the appropriate type of assessment you need to design that will provide you with that evidence.

Exhibit 5.3 English Course Example of Summative and Formative Assessments

Outcomes	Summative Assessments	Formative Assessments
Apply the writing process to create effective writing products such as papers and presentations.	Final writing product Artifacts of writing process, for example, brainstorms, outline, annotated references, drafts	• Self-assessment • Quiz • Audience analysis • Annotated bibliography • Outline • Draft paper • Peer review
Adhere to conventions of standard written English to effectively communicate ideas.	Final writing product	• Self-assessment • Quiz • Annotated bibliography • Draft paper • Tutor review
Apply appropriate form and style to clearly and concisely present ideas.	Final writing product	• Self-assessment • Quiz • Format writing sample • Annotated bibliography • Argument analysis worksheet • Tutor review
Integrate critical thinking strategies to provide logical arguments and adequate support for ideas to persuade target audience.	Final writing product	• Self-assessment • Quiz • Audience analysis • Annotated bibliography • Research analysis worksheet

In this chapter, we looked at how to design assessments up front in the course development process to ensure you are providing learners with appropriate opportunities to demonstrate their progress toward and achievement of the learning outcomes. Using this approach you will have a clear understanding of the evidence you will need to understand the extent to which learners have met each of the outcomes, which will inform the instructional strategies you design later on. With your assessments in hand, we now move to creating a course sequence and structure to support the course design.

Action Steps

To help you apply the concepts in this chapter, complete the following:

- Brainstorm summative and formative assessment strategies for your course learning outcomes. While you think through your assessment options, keep coming back to your learning outcomes to make sure you are providing appropriate opportunities for learners to demonstrate their progress toward and achievement of the learning outcomes. Review exhibits 5.1 and 5.2 for assessment ideas.
- Review your assessments and think about what you learned about your learning outcomes as you started designing them. Consider the following questions:
  - Did you realize that the focus of your learning outcomes is different than what you initially thought?
  - Did you find that there were competencies that needed more emphasis than you originally thought?
- Review the ramifications of your assessment design on your learning outcomes and competencies and take some time to clarify the wording based on your work. You may also find that your initial outcomes were not accurate enough, so feel free to go back and make adjustments at this time before you move further into the design process.
- Review your outcomes and assessment drafts and make sure you are providing appropriate opportunities for learners to demonstrate their accomplishment of the outcomes in summative assessments and get feedback on their progress with formative assessments. If necessary, create additional formative assessment opportunities to ensure learners receive adequate feedback prior to summative assessments.
- Consider sharing your assessment ideas with instructors, leaders, or learners to get another perspective on the alignment of the assessments to your learning outcomes and the educational goals of your learners.

Sequence of Instruction

OBJECTIVES

After reviewing this chapter, you should be able to

- Analyze learners' entering knowledge, skills, and attitudes in relation to your course learning outcomes to determine a starting point for your instruction.
- Create a sequence of instruction for the course based on a developmental path from learners' starting points to achieving the course learning outcomes and competencies by the end of the course.

Now that you've developed the outcomes for your online course and determined appropriate assessments that will provide evidence for the degree to which learners have met the course learning outcomes, it's time to determine an appropriate structure and sequence for learning. Determining this structure at this point helps you to continue to define learners' path from entering skills, knowledge, and attitudes to a higher level of achievement by the end of the course. Delving deeper into this developmental pathway helps you lay the groundwork for the instructional strategies you will develop to help learners successfully demonstrate progress and achievement of outcomes. At this point, you may be tempted to jump ahead to select a textbook and start to structure the course based on the chapter structure of the text. This sequence of chapters, however, may or may not be the best for learners to achieve the course competencies. It is good to remember that textbook writers had their own goals and thought processes in place when sequencing a text that may not support or may even be in conflict with the goals for your course. Instead, for this task, you will continue to examine the relationships among your outcomes as well as your assessments and how they may be appropriately sequenced for your learners.

STARTING POINT FOR INSTRUCTION

Traditional instructional design has many different prescriptions for sequencing options from familiar to unknown, by difficulty, by process, from simple to complex, and many other options. Many authors have also written about specific instances when each of these approaches is applicable. Rather than going through rules and different prescriptions, however, you really want to think about structure and sequencing from a developmental perspective for your learners. You want to focus the course structure on leading learners from their current knowledge and skill level through a path to successfully achieve all the learning outcomes. Because you developed course learning outcomes, you already know the end point of the course. Now, you want to go back to your audience analysis and establish a starting point for your learners and develop the path to achieving the learning outcomes by the end of the course. Some of these different sequencing options will come into play once we start laying out that path.

First, examine your audience analysis again and think about the prerequisite skills and knowledge learners may or may not have coming into your course. Also, think through any potential misunderstandings learners may have before they come to your course. These could be the aha moments your learners have had in the past when they struggled and struggled until they realized something key to their understanding.

Exhibit 6.1 shows how you can begin to organize your thoughts using the example of the English course. Start with the second column and list each of the course outcomes and associated competencies. Then, use the first column to list the associated incoming knowledge and skills of learners. As you consider

Exhibit 6.1 Learners' Entering Knowledge, Skills, and Attitudes

Learners' Entering Knowledge, Skills, and Attitudes	Learning Outcomes and Competencies
• At least basic level reading skills • Variety of writing skill levels and experience with the writing process • May have some knowledge of how to identify information needs and locate appropriate sources	Apply writing process to create effective writing products such as papers and presentations. • Use brainstorming and outlining strategies to initiate writing process. • Locate scholarly and practitioner resources appropriate to the audience and writing purpose. • Use drafting and revising strategies to refine writing products (papers and presentations). • Proofread papers and presentations to correct grammar, mechanics, and usage issues.
• Variety of knowledge and application of standard written English conventions • ESL learners may have difficulty with English conventions.	Adhere to conventions of standard written English to effectively communicate ideas. • Use appropriate capitalization and punctuation. • Use appropriate sentence structure. • Follow grammar rules including tenses and subject-verb agreement. • Spellcheck work and correct any misspellings.
• Little to no knowledge and application of format and style for college-level writing and real-world writing products	Apply appropriate form and style to clearly and concisely present ideas. • Use appropriate paper structure based on relevant style guide. • Cite references appropriately in text and at the end of the paper in a reference list or bibliography according to a style guide. • Use appropriate headings.
• Little to no formal critical thinking experience	Integrate critical thinking strategies to provide logical arguments and adequate support for ideas to persuade target audience. • Practice using a critical thinking model to evaluate and construct arguments. • Develop logical arguments using proper support. • Adapt communication to specific audiences.

learners' incoming knowledge and skills, consider the prerequisite knowledge, skills, and attitudes related to the outcomes you are expecting learners to have when they begin your course. Be sure to review any formal prerequisite courses or curriculum as you determine learners' entering knowledge, skills, and attitudes.

SEQUENCING STRATEGIES

Now, that you see the starting and end points for your learners, you can determine an appropriate sequence of instruction to meet the intended learning outcomes. Depending on the relationships among your outcomes, you may consider a number of different ways to sequence instruction including from simple to complex, known to unknown, depending on instruction, or based on a sequence of events.

Simple to complex: One sequencing strategy is to begin with simple concepts, tasks, or skills and move to more complex ones.

Known to unknown: Another sequencing strategy is moving from familiar topics to less familiar ones.

Dependent: You may also need to sequence your instruction based on dependencies of the outcomes.

Sequence of events: Finally, you may sequence instruction based on a chronological order such as a historical event or steps in a process.

For the English course example, a dual-sequencing approach is used. First, the course starts with simple to complex by starting with writing conventions, then a critical thinking model, and then the writing process. To further break down the sequence, the sequence of events strategy is used for the writing process section of the course. Exhibit 6.2 shows a table with rows that start to break down the topics of the course and sequence them appropriately.

Exhibit 6.2 Course Sequence for English Writing Course

Starting Point
- Variety of writing skill levels and experience with the writing process
- Variety of knowledge and application of standard written English conventions
- Little to no knowledge and application of format and style for college-level writing and real-world writing products
- Little to no formal critical thinking experience
- At least basic level reading skills
- May have some knowledge of how to identify information needs and locate appropriate sources

Writing Conventions

Sentence structure:
- Capitalization and punctuation
- Follow grammar rules including tenses and subject-verb agreement
- Spellcheck work and correct any misspellings
- Paragraph structure

Critical Thinking
- Critical thinking model
- Arguments

Exhibit 6.2 (*continued*)

Writing Process
- Audience analysis
- Brainstorm
- Outline
- Research
- Draft
- Revision
- Editing

Form and Style
- Formatting
- Style guides
- Proofreading

Final Assessment of Outcomes
1. Apply writing process to create effective writing products such as papers and presentations.
   a. Use brainstorming and outlining strategies to initiate the writing process.
   b. Locate scholarly and practitioner resources appropriate to the audience and writing purpose.
   c. Use drafting and revising strategies to refine writing products (papers and presentations).
   d. Proofread papers and presentations to correct grammar, mechanics, and usage issues.
2. Adhere to conventions of standard written English to effectively communicate ideas.
   a. Use appropriate capitalization and punctuation.
   b. Use appropriate sentence structure.
   c. Follow grammar rules including tenses and subject-verb agreement.
   d. Spellcheck work and correct any misspellings.
3. Apply appropriate form and style to clearly and concisely present ideas.
   a. Use appropriate paper structure based on a relevant style guide.
   b. Cite references appropriately in the text and at the end of the paper in a reference list or bibliography according to a style guide.
   c. Use appropriate headings.
4. Integrate critical thinking strategies to provide logical arguments and adequate support for ideas to persuade target audience.
   a. Practice using a critical thinking model to evaluate and construct arguments.
   b. Develop logical arguments using proper support.
   c. Adapt communication to specific audiences

SEQUENCING ASSESSMENTS

Once you have your sequence determined, you can start to see where your assessments will fall within the structure and sequence of the course. Start with your summative assessments and determine how they are related to your topics and when you would want them due. Then, move on to sequencing your formative assessments. These become your outcome milestones because they provide learners with feedback on their progress toward the final course outcomes. Exhibit 6.3 illustrates how the English course's formative and summative assessments have been integrated within the sequence of instruction.

Exhibit 6.3 Course Sequence of English Writing Course with Milestone Assessments

Major Topics	Subtopics	Formative Assessments	Summative Assessments
Introduction		Self-assessment of current writing knowledge	
	Purpose of writing in different fields of practice		
	Examples of strong writing		
Writing conventions	Sentence structure: • Capitalization and punctuation • Follow grammar rules including tenses and subject-verb agreement. • Spellcheck work and correct any misspellings.		
	Paragraph structure		
		Quiz—writing conventions	
Critical thinking		Self-assessment of critical thinking skills	
	Critical thinking model		
	Arguments		
		Quiz—critical thinking	
Writing process		Self-assessment	
	Audience analysis	Audience analysis assignment	
	Brainstorm		
	Outline	Draft outline	
	Research • Annotated bibliography	• Research analysis worksheet • Annotated bibliography	
	Draft	Peer review	
	Revision	Tutor review	
	Editing		
Format and style	Format standards		
	Style guides	Format and style quiz	
	Proofreading		
			Final paper

In this chapter, we discussed how to create an effective structure and sequence of instruction based on the intended learning outcomes and associated knowledge, skills, and attitudes required to attain the course outcomes. As you continue through the design process, you might find yourself reordering elements and activities. This is completely natural as you start to dig further into the instructional activities learners will engage in to achieve those outcomes. In the next few chapters, you will delve into instructional strategies as you continue to design the instruction for your course. The design of your instructional strategies will provide your learners with meaningful activities that will help them make progress toward the course learning outcomes and prepare them for the assessments you just laid out in this chapter. This will help you further refine your course structure and continue to design the course to support high achievement and persistence.

Action Steps

To apply the concepts in this chapter, complete the following:

- Determine the starting point for your instruction based on your understanding of your learners' prerequisite knowledge, skills, and attitudes.
- Create a sequence of instruction for the course based on a developmental path from learners' starting points to achieving the course learning outcomes and competencies by the end of the course.
- Sequence your formative and summative assessments. Review exhibits 6.2 and 6.3 for examples of how to structure this work.

PART 4

Design of Instructional Strategies

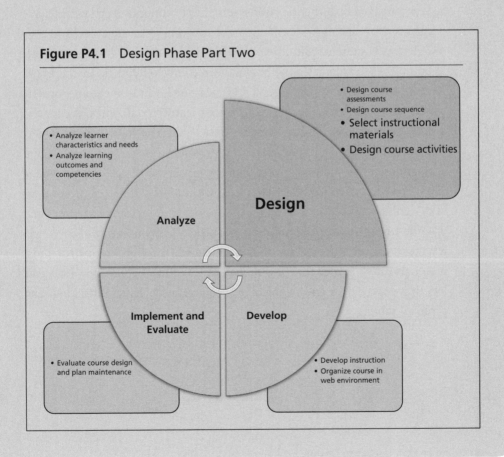

Figure P4.1 Design Phase Part Two

- Analyze learner characteristics and needs
- Analyze learning outcomes and competencies

Analyze

- Design course assessments
- Design course sequence
- Select instructional materials
- Design course activities

Design

- Evaluate course design and plan maintenance

Implement and Evaluate

Develop

- Develop instruction
- Organize course in web environment

Let's take a moment to recap the course design process so far. In part 2, we considered important factors and conducted an analysis that helped you understand your online learners and their needs and completed a brainstorming activity in which you visually developed a list of knowledge, skills, and attitudes that will need to be addressed in the course you are developing. From this exercise, you developed outcomes and related competencies. In part 3, you began the design phase by designing assessments to demonstrate the degree to which learners will have met the learning outcomes of your course. Then, you considered the sequence of instruction for your course. Instructional design is an iterative process, so along the way, you may have revised some of these steps as you progressed.

In part 4, we continue the design phase and design instructional strategies and activities to support the achievement of the course learning outcomes. In chapter 7, "Foundations of Transformative Learning," we discuss important learning principles and instructional strategies to ensure your learners are actively engaged in authentic course activities to support deep learning. We discuss active learning and how cognitive learning styles affect learning. We also discuss cognitive scaffolding strategies to ensure your learners are able to complete learning activities and achieve course outcomes. In chapter 8, "Selection of Instructional Materials," we discuss how to choose appropriate course materials that align with your course learning outcomes. We look at different types of text-based and media-based materials that can help learners understand key concepts and skills and provide strategies for locating and evaluating course materials to support your course design. In chapter 9, "Design of Effective Course Activities," we lead you through the process of designing instructional activities to support your learning outcomes and provide various examples that may be used in your online course to help learners turn the information they have gained through the instructional materials into knowledge. We also look at activities that provide authentic learning experiences and enabled rich engagement, critical thinking, and problem solving.

7

Foundations of Transformative Learning

OBJECTIVES

After reviewing this chapter, you should be able to

- Incorporate active learning strategies to create engaging and motivating learning experiences for your learners.
- Develop presence through your course design to engage learners and support their persistence.
- Align instructional strategies to individual learning styles by integrating a variety of active learning strategies in the course design.
- Integrate different types of cognitive scaffolding to support learners' successful achievement of course learning outcomes.

Instructional strategies should enable and facilitate learning so the learner can achieve maximum success. Prior to beginning the design of your instructional strategies, it's important to have an understanding of some theoretical foundations that affect their design. Understanding how to design active learning strategies helps you create an engaging learning experience. In addition, in order to involve learners and help them persist in the online environment, it is critical to understand how to develop presence in your online course. If learners don't feel a connection with you and their peers, it is difficult for them to persist online. It's also important that your instructional strategies help learners persist by matching different learning styles with the types of activities learners participate in. Using instructional strategies that help learners to efficiently and effectively achieve the learning outcomes for the course develops learner self-efficacy and intellectual development as well as aids academic integration.

PRINCIPLES OF LEARNING

Understanding how learning occurs supports the creation of effective and engaging learning experiences that help individuals succeed in their studies. The emerging field of learning sciences brings together crossfunctional research related to cognition and learning to provide key insights about how people learn and how to design with learning in mind. In *How People Learn* (Bransford, Brown, & Cocking, 2000), three hallmarks of the science of learning are put forth based on research to date about how people learn. These hallmarks include learning with understanding, the role of preexisting knowledge in the learning process, and active learning and metacognition.

Learning with understanding focuses on the idea of learning "usable knowledge" in a network of meaning organized by important concepts. This idea is based on research about how experts organize their knowledge and how learners should be able to understand and use the knowledge they learn in different contexts rather than remember large bodies of disconnected facts. This includes understanding the facts, why they are important, relationships to other facts and knowledge, and when to use them.

The role of preexisting knowledge is immensely important for the processes of learning. There is an understanding that learners come into the education environment with a wide range of previous experiences, knowledge, skills, and attitudes that influence the way they construct new meanings. Research indicates that activating this previous knowledge and using it as a foundation to build new knowledge improves learning outcomes. This is especially relevant to adult learners who have many more years of experiences, knowledge, and even potential misconceptions related to learning outcomes.

Finally, active learning is a central hallmark of learning. Active learning places the responsibility of learning on the learner. It requires learners to reflect on what they know as they actively engage in reading, writing, dialogue, and reflection to make meaning from the content and construct knowledge. Active learning invites learners to process, apply, interact, and share experiences as part of their learning. This can motivate learners by helping them understand the relevance of ideas presented in the course in relationship to the real world. Active learning also has a positive impact on persistence because it encourages self-direction. Active learning strategies can be transformative because they focus on meaning making that is relevant to the learner rather than learning for the sake of meeting course objectives. It is grounded in constructivist learning principles, which focus on engaging learners in critical thinking and collaborative learning opportunities to construct knowledge. This requires the learner to develop strong critical thinking skills and understand how to engage with other learners to share perspectives and create meaning.

Because this model positions learning and learners at the center of activities, the key questions become what do learners need to know, believe, and do and what activities will help them achieve those outcomes rather than focusing on what you need to teach your learners. Activity design focuses on supporting learners to critically analyze and apply new concepts and skills and integrate new learning with their previous experiences, knowledge, and skills. In *How People Learn*, the authors focus on the ability of learners to engage in metacognition to assess, monitor, and adjust strategies during learning as key to active learning.

The authors use this research and these concepts to outline three key findings for aligning learning with the research about how people learn: "we need to engage learners' preconceptions when designing activities to ensure they grasp new knowledge and skills; . . . to develop competence, learners need a foundation of facts in a framework organized for learning and transfer; . . . metacognitive approaches to instruction help learners take control of their learning" (pp. 14–18).

By integrating best practices based on research about how people learn, we can design more effective learning activities that help learners achieve success in their learning outcomes and build confidence in their skills.

ENGAGEMENT IN THE ONLINE ENVIRONMENT

Another important instructional strategy is the development of presence in the online environment, which is essential for active learning strategies. In addition, the lack of it can cause learners to drop out (Bean & Metzner, 1985; Rovai,

2003; Tinto, 1975; Workman & Stenard, 1996). Research indicates that the more learners can develop relationships with other learners and the instructor, the greater satisfaction they will have, which can improve the likelihood of the learner persisting in a program of study. Interaction is related to learner perception of presence, which is a predictor of learner satisfaction in computer-mediated environments (Picciano, 2002).

Garrison, Anderson, and Archer (2001) developed a community of inquiry model to support engagement in an online environment to achieve educational goals. They propose that learning is more than interactions among participants and should be embedded within a community of inquiry that provides opportunities for the development of cognitive presence, social presence, and teaching presence.

Cognitive Presence

Cognitive presence is "the extent to which the participants in any particular configuration of a community of inquiry are able to construct meaning" (Garrison, Anderson, & Archer, 2001, p. 89). Cognitive presence supports discourse and is necessary for learners to think critically. It is important to recognize that cognitive presence focuses on higher-order thinking processes as opposed to specific individual learning outcomes (Garrison, Anderson, & Archer, 2001). Critical thinking skills are necessary for learners to engage in a community of inquiry to construct knowledge and reason through concepts and ideas. High-level cognitive skills needed to think critically can be developed and integrated in instructional activities to help learners develop critical inquiry.

Social Presence

The second element, social presence, is defined as "the ability of participants in a community of inquiry to project their personal characteristics into the community, thereby presenting themselves to the other participants as 'real people'" (Garrison, Anderson, & Archer, 2001, p. 89). Social presence supports cognitive presence by facilitating the development of peer relationships to develop trust and a sense of belonging. The more learners are able to establish themselves with other learners and the instructor, the more trust they will build. Trust helps learners feel comfortable with sharing their thoughts and ideas without the fear of being wrong or being criticized. As the level of interaction increases, a greater sense of community can occur where learners can comfortably share their divergent thoughts and perspectives to construct knowledge and understanding.

Teaching Presence

The third element is teaching presence, which can be performed by the instructor, a teaching assistant, or any other participant in the community. Teaching presence is critical in facilitating interactions to help learners develop social presence and cognitive presence. The role of teaching presence also includes the design of the course and the instructional strategies you choose to support social and cognitive presence. In addition strategies to facilitate learning including providing direct instruction, focusing the discussion on specific issues, summarizing the discussion, confirming understanding, diagnosing misperceptions, injecting knowledge from diverse sources, and responding to technical concerns develop teaching presence and support learning.

The development of presence in the online environment is essential for learning to occur and the lack of it can cause learners to become dissatisfied and eventually drop out. Cognitive presence, social presence, and teaching presence are critical building blocks that can support online learners as they engage in the online environment to achieve their educational goals. In the upcoming chapters we will describe specific strategies to support the development of a community of inquiry in the course.

COGNITIVE LEARNING STYLES

Before you begin designing your instructional strategies, it's important to understand how an individual's cognitive styles will affect his or her learning. *Cognitive style* refers to "an individual's characteristic and consistent approach to organizing and processing information" (Tennant, 1997, p. 80). There are numerous classifications of these styles; however, a dominant approach is the Kolb Learning Style Inventory (LSI) (Kolb, 1976). Having an understanding of how individuals learn will help you choose appropriate instructional strategies to support the needs of all learners.

The LSI (Kolb, 1999) measures cognitive style preferences on two bipolar dimensions: active experimentation versus reflective observation, and concrete versus abstract. The LSI identifies learners' preference for each of these four

Exhibit 7.1 Learning Activities Based on Kolb's Learning Preferences

Style	Preferences	Activities
Accommodators	• Prefer concrete experiences • Prefer active experimentation • Have the ability to carry out plans and get things done	• Hands-on or trial-and-error methods • Open-ended problems • Learner presentations • Design projects • Subjective exams • Simulations
Divergers	• Prefer concrete experiences to help them understand ideas and concepts • Use experience and knowledge to reflect and see different perspectives • Are open-minded • Have difficulty making decisions • May prefer to observe rather than participate	• Case study videos • Peer interaction • Motivational stories • Group discussion • Group projects • Subjective tests
Assimilators	• Prefer high levels of abstract conceptualization and reflective observation • Good at taking in a wide range of information and reducing it to a more logical form • Like to plan and define problems • Prefer theoretical models and deductive reasoning	• Independent projects • Lectures • Textbook reading • Demonstration by instructor • Objective exams • Concept maps • Simulations
Convergers	• Prefer high levels of abstract conceptualization • Need opportunities for active experimentation • Prefer to learn via problem solving, deductive decision making, and direct application of ideas and theories • Prefer to solve problems using hypothetical reasoning	• Independent projects • Problem-solving exercises • Simulations • Demonstrations

Source: (Stavredes, 2011).

learning strategies, and the combination of the scores from the two scales identifies learners' preferred style as *diverger, converger, assimilator,* or *accommodator.* Exhibit 7.1 shows the preferences of different styles and the activities that fit each learning style.

Learning Style Preferences

Learners identified as accommodators or divergers rely heavily on concrete experience. Learners in the accommodator category combine this with a preference for active experimentation and have the ability to carry out plans and get things done. In addition, accommodators like hands-on or trial-and-error methods of learning. Divergers prefer a combination of concrete experience and reflective observation. They are characterized as open-minded and they look at a learning situation from many different perspectives. They often have difficulty making a decision and may prefer to observe rather than participate. Learners falling into the assimilator and converger types share a preference for high levels of abstract conceptualization. Assimilators prefer to combine abstract conceptualization with reflective observation and are good at taking in a wide range of information and reducing it to a more logical form. Assimilators like to plan and define problems; they tend to prefer theoretical models and deductive reasoning, as well as abstract concepts and ideas, over interaction with other people. Convergers combine this preference with a need for active experimentation, and they prefer to learn via problem solving, deductive decision making, and the direct application of ideas and theories.

Instructional Strategies for Different Learning Style Preferences

An understanding of learning styles can help you develop appropriate instructional strategies for your online course. Accommodator strategies focus on experimentation with hands-on or trial-and-error methods such as problem-solving activities. Divergers learn best by being presented with concrete information to help them understand ideas and concepts and then use their experience and knowledge to reflect on and see different perspectives. These styles can be accommodated by using real-world problems. Divergers also prefer instructional methods that include peer interaction because they are interested in the perspectives of other learners. Divergers use these different perspectives to challenge their own thinking and adjust their initial reflection of the experience. Assimilators prefer theoretical models and deductive reasoning. Enabling them to work independently with information can help them to define a problem and develop a plan. Another tool that can be used is concept mapping to enable assimilators to manipulate concepts in visual presentations to show connections or simulations so they can build and test models. Finally, convergers prefer working on projects that enable them to plan and organize information and use their hypothetical reasoning skills to solve problems. It's important to understand that the goal is not to cater to individual learning styles but to provide a variety of instructional strategies that meet different styles as well as enable learners to develop new learning styles as they engage in new learning experiences.

COGNITIVE SCAFFOLDING STRATEGIES

As we have already discussed, cognitive learning styles have an impact on learning; however, we can support learning by developing appropriate support in the form of cognitive scaffolding to help learners and ensure they are able to engage fully and successfully complete course activities. Many learners drop out because they hit a wall and can't progress in a course. In the online environment, where learners are separated from the instructor and other learners, it is more difficult to progress in their studies when faced with issues and questions, which intensifies the issue. As you develop your instructional strategies, the concept of scaffolding will help you develop a learning experience that supports all learners in your course regardless of their prior knowledge, thinking and learning skills, and styles of learning.

Cognitive scaffolding is based on Lev Vygotsky's sociocultural theory (1978), which describes the zone of proximal development. Vygotsky studied individual development and advanced the idea of a "zone of proximal development," which is "the distance between the actual developmental level as determined by independent problem-solving and the level of potential development as determined through problem-solving under adult guidance or in collaboration with more capable peers" (p. 86).

Cognitive scaffolding is meant to support learners in this zone—in the gap between what they are able to accomplish on their own and what they can accomplish with the assistance of an individual with more advanced knowledge and skills or tools to help them work on their own without the need of another person. The key to incorporating cognitive scaffolding strategies is to use the right amount of scaffolding to support learners in their zone of proximal development. Dabbagh (2003) writes, "too much scaffolding could result in dampening students' efforts to actively pursue their learning goals, causing them to lose their momentum or drive towards meaning making and self-directed learning efforts, and too little scaffolding could result in students' inability to successfully complete or perform certain tasks and instructional activities, leading to anxiety, frustration, and finally loss of motivation and attrition" (p. 40).

The term *scaffolding* is used because the idea is that over time, learners will not need the scaffolding. Ultimately, if applied over time, this helps learners to become self-regulated learners able to motivate themselves, plan their learning process, assess their progress and adjust strategies, and locate and use resources to support their learning (Schunk & Zimmerman, 1994).

Hannafin, Land, and Oliver (1999) consider four different types of scaffolding: conceptual, metacognitive, procedural, and strategic. Stavredes (2011) went on to define these types of scaffolding for the online environment. *Procedural scaffolding* guides learners about how to use resources, tools, and other elements within the online learning environment. *Metacognitive scaffolding* helps guide learners about how to think. In particular, it guides learners to help them develop a plan for learning, strategies for monitoring themselves as they learn, and specific ways to evaluate their learning at the end of an activity. *Conceptual scaffolding* guides learners to help them work through complex problems and identify key concepts and ideas related to the task at hand. The last type of scaffolding, *strategic scaffolding*, is used by the instructor to provide just-in-time help to individual learners who have difficulty learning online.

The use of scaffolding can provide important support to help build learners' academic skills and help them develop greater confidence in their ability to successfully learn, which has a tremendous impact on persistence. In chapter 3, we discussed the importance of understanding learners and the issues they have that can affect their ability to persist, such as a lack of time management, information literacy, or writing skills. Scaffolding techniques can be used to overcome some of the issues we discussed in that chapter.

Procedural Scaffolding

Procedural scaffolding guides learners as they figure out how to navigate the course environment and engage in learning activities. Learners may have difficulty understanding what to do when they begin an online course. This difficulty is compounded if the online course is not built with a standard design template, because learners must orient themselves to a new navigation structure and location of resources for each new online course. In addition, they have to learn how the content is delivered, how the units of study are structured, what the expectations are for engaging in the course, as well as other features unique to the course. You can eliminate unnecessary frustration and anxiety by scaffolding the learning environment to help learners understand what to do once they begin the course and how to engage with you, the content, and their peers. Procedural scaffolding can help learners persist in learning by orienting them to the course, helping them understand the expectations for engaging in your course, and identifying processes, resources, and tools that will be used throughout the course.

Metacognitive Scaffolding

Metacognitive scaffolding supports learners in developing thinking skills to manage their learning. Learners who have never been to college, have been away from college for a number of years, or who have never developed strong thinking skills will benefit from scaffolding to build these skills as they engage in learning activities. Learners who do not have well-developed thinking skills struggle more in learning, which makes them extremely vulnerable to dropping out. Metacognitive scaffolding supports planning, monitoring, and evaluating processes to support learners as they engage in learning to ensure they are processing information efficiently and effectively for storage and retrieval. As learners become more aware of their thinking, they can act on this awareness and learn better (Bransford, Brown, & Cocking, 1999). Metacognitive strategies for monitoring learning include tracking information about how learners are progressing, whether learners are on the right track and attending to the correct goals, and the potential outcomes of their efforts (Hannafin, Land, & Oliver, 1999). There are several scaffolding strategies that can assist learners in monitoring their progress. Study guides and worksheets are effective tools to help learners monitor their understanding. These tools can keep learners focused on the components of a specific task as well as the order in which tasks should be completed.

Conceptual Scaffolding

Conceptual scaffolding guides learners about what to consider during learning. If learners have difficulty understanding course concepts, they can become frustrated and lose motivation. Conceptual scaffolding can support learners as they engage in difficult content by helping them identify key conceptual knowledge and organize it into meaningful structures that support learning (Hannifin, Land, & Oliver, 1999). Strategies include the use of advance organizers, graphical organizers, and outlines. As you design your course content, consider ways to introduce major topics and help learners understand how they interrelate.

David Ausubel proposed the use of advance organizers to scaffold the learning of new information (Ausubel, 1960). Advance organizers help learners link prior knowledge with new information. An example of an advance organizer is presenting a summary of the main ideas in a reading passage and explaining content at a "higher level of abstraction, generality, and inclusiveness than the reading itself" (Ausubel, 1963, p. 81). It differs from an overview in that it relates content to learners' current cognitive structure, thus enriching existing understanding and enabling learners to link prior knowledge with new concepts. When new information is presented to learners, they use prior knowledge to make sense of new information. Learners who have little prior knowledge of a subject may comprehend incoming information inefficiently because they have not developed mental structures to store new information about the topic. A goal of teaching is to simplify the information or elaborate on the information to help learners activate or build appropriate mental structures to organize and interpret the incoming information, which aids in recall.

Strategic Scaffolding

Strategic scaffolding tailors instruction to support individual learners, which requires you to understand individual learning preferences and levels of prior knowledge in order to help them meet the intended outcomes of the course. For novice learners, cognitive overload may be an issue; strategies to help simplify the content and organize the information into discrete chunks will help learners process the information more effectively. Alternative explanations can help learners understand concepts by helping them see other ways of looking at the ideas being presented. Probing questions can provide explicit strategic clues for learners who need a place to begin; such questions can also be used in the middle of a problem-solving activity to help learners overcome barriers in order to persist in an activity. Sometimes learners will need hints to understand the next step in a process or activity, or worked examples to understand the expectations of an activity to give them a starting point. Worked examples can also support learners by providing them a way to think through a process to solve a problem. The key is to present worked examples that enable learners to generalize from the example to new problems. Supplementary resources can also help learners strategically to accomplish a learning task by supporting gaps in skills or knowledge.

For more information on cognitive scaffolding strategies and a full range of scaffolding templates, consult *Effective Online Teaching: Foundations and Strategies for Student Success* (Stavredes, 2011). In addition, in the upcoming chapters, we describe different examples of scaffolding strategies to support your online learners.

In this chapter, we have laid the foundation of important concepts and theories that help you develop instructional strategies to support the delivery of a transformative learning experience. In the upcoming chapters, we explore a number of instructional activities to support the ideas presented in this chapter.

Action Steps

To help you apply the concepts in this chapter, complete the following:

- As you progress through the upcoming chapters on course materials and instructional strategies consider the following:
  - Are the strategies active?
  - Do the strategies encourage social presence?
  - Do the strategies develop cognitive presence and engage learners in a community of inquiry?
  - Do the strategies encourage teaching presence?
  - Do the instructional strategies meet the needs of learners' cognitive learning styles?
  - Do the scaffolding strategies ensure all learners can successfully complete the course activities?
- Come back to this chapter later in your development to review how you are addressing these foundational concepts and continue to make adjustments to ensure you have incorporated them in the design of your online course.

Selection of Instructional Materials

OBJECTIVES

After reviewing this chapter, you should be able to

- Select a variety of high-quality materials to support learners' achievement of learning outcomes and competencies.
- Select multimedia that adheres to principles to ensure that media supports learning and greater comprehension and recall.
- Evaluate instructional materials to ensure quality, relevance to learners, and alignment to the course learning outcomes.
- Evaluate instructional materials to ensure compliance with copyright and accessibility principles.

Now it's time to choose appropriate instructional activities. When using an outcomes-based course design process, instructional materials take on a slightly different purpose. In this design process, rather than the book driving the outcomes and course structure, you began by determining the outcomes and aligning assessments to outcomes that demonstrate their achievement. Then you choose appropriate instructional materials to support the course learning outcomes. Course materials take on the purpose of supporting learners' achievement

Exhibit 8.1 Instructional Materials Selection

Outcomes and Competencies	Assessments	Instructional Material (Align all instructional materials to the course outcomes)
1. Apply the writing process to create effective writing products such as papers and presentations. a. Use brainstorming and outlining strategies to initiate the writing process. b. Locate scholarly and practitioner resources appropriate to the audience and writing purpose. c. Use drafting and revising strategies to refine writing products (papers and presentations). d. Proofread papers and presentations to correct grammar, mechanics, and usage issues.	Final writing product: • Artifacts of writing process, for example, brainstorms, outline, annotated references, drafts • Self-assessment • Quiz • Audience analysis • Annotated bibliography • Outline • Draft paper • Peer review	Hacker, D., & Sommers, N. (2011). *A writer's reference with strategies for online learners* (7th ed.). New York: Macmillan. Purdue Online Writing Lab. *The writing process.* Retrieved from http://owl.english.purdue.edu /owl/section/1/1 Library resources for locating appropriate resources for writing products Peer review checklist Audience analysis worksheet Exemplar writing products from past courses A writing process video
2. Adhere to conventions of standard written English to effectively communicate ideas. a. Use appropriate capitalization and punctuation. b. Use appropriate sentence structure. c. Follow grammar rules including tenses and subject-verb agreement. d. Spellcheck work and correct any misspellings.	Final writing product: • Self-assessment • Quiz • Annotated bibliography • Draft paper • Tutor review	Hacker, D., & Sommers, N. (2011). *A writer's reference with strategies for online learners* (7th ed.). New York: Macmillan. Purdue Online Writing Lab. *Mechanics.* Retrieved from http://owl.english.purdue.edu/owl /section/1/4 Purdue Online Writing Lab. *Punctuation.* Retrieved from http://owl.english.purdue.edu /owl/section/1/6 Purdue Online Writing Lab. *Grammar.* Retrieved from http://owl.english.purdue.edu /owl/section/1/5
3. Apply appropriate form and style to clearly and concisely present ideas. a. Use appropriate paper structure based on relevant style guide. b. Cite references appropriately in text and at the end of the paper in a reference list or bibliography according to a style guide. c. Use appropriate headings.	Final writing product: • Self-assessment • Quiz • Format writing sample • Annotated bibliography • Argument analysis worksheet • Tutor review	American Psychological Association. (2010). *Publication manual of the American Psychological Association* (6th ed.). Washington, DC: Author. American Psychological Association. *APA style blog.* Retrieved from http://blog.apastyle.org American Psychological Association. *APA style.* Retrieved from www.apastyle.org APA templates for different types of writing products APA style and format checklist

Exhibit 8.1 (*continued*)

Outcomes and Competencies	Assessments	Instructional Material (Align all instructional materials to the course outcomes)
4. Integrate critical thinking strategies to provide logical arguments and adequate support for ideas to persuade target audience. a. Practice using a critical thinking model to evaluate and construct arguments. b. Develop logical arguments using proper support. c. Adapt communication to specific audiences.	Final writing product: • Self-assessment • Quiz • Audience analysis • Annotated bibliography • Research analysis worksheet	Paul, R., & Elder, L. (2009). *Miniature guide to critical thinking: Concepts and tools.* Dillon Beach, CA: Foundation for Critical Thinking. Audience analysis worksheet Research analysis worksheet Worked example of logical argument

of outcomes by gaining knowledge related to course outcomes, modeling expert performance, providing inputs for course activities, and much more.

As you progress through choosing appropriate instructional materials, you will need a way to ensure the materials you pick align to the assessment strategies as evidence that learners have achieved the course outcomes. As you select the course materials, use the instructional material selection table (exhibit 8.1) to align your instructional materials with the course outcomes and assessments. Begin by listing your learning outcomes and assessments and as you review resources, list them under the appropriate outcome or outcomes, so you can carefully track resources and fill gaps along the way to ensure your instructional materials cover all knowledge, skills, and attitudes needed for the learning outcomes. Exhibit 8.1 provides an example of some initial instructional material ideas for our English 101 example.

As you begin to review instructional materials, you want to choose different ways to present information to ensure learners are mentally active as they perceive, process, consolidate, consider, and judge information (Horton, 2012). We will discuss a variety of text-based and multimedia instructional materials to support learning through the use of multiple representations of information, which can support the individual learning styles discussed in chapter 7.

TEXT-BASED INSTRUCTIONAL MATERIALS

There are a number of different types of text-based course materials you can select for your online course. The main two types are textbooks and articles.

Textbooks

If you would like to use a textbook, consider connecting with representatives from publishing companies for help finding appropriate resources for the course. Often, institutions work with specific representatives from different companies. You can send publishing representatives a list of the course outcomes and ask them to map specific textbooks to the outcomes you have provided. This will save you time in trying to find them yourself and most publishers are more than happy to do this for you. Another reason to work with the major publishing representatives is that they will know if a textbook is in revision or about to go into revision. That will save you a lot of wasted effort if you happen to choose a textbook that is in revision and then you find out months later that the textbook has been completely rewritten and you need to do a major edit to the course or choose another textbook. Additionally, ensure that you are using enough of the textbook to justify the cost to the learner. We discussed the connections between financial issues and persistence in chapter 3. We have found many learners fail to engage in an online course because they can't afford to purchase their textbooks and they end up getting too far behind to catch up. These issues may be exacerbated by high materials costs for the course, so keep that in mind as you are choosing your instructional materials. If you find several textbooks from the same publisher with relevant content to meet the course learning outcomes, ask if they can create a custom textbook for you. With digital texts, this is quite easy for them to do and can end up saving learners money by not having to purchase each of the books separately.

Articles

In addition to textbooks, you want to be sure to review the resources available in your institution's library. Often, the library has purchased thousands of articles and texts that do not cost your learners anything extra to use. Often, librarians can help you locate appropriate materials available in their collection for the course. There are also many professional organizations and publications online that provide free resources to individuals in the field and can help learners engage in authentic content related to their fields.

OPEN EDUCATIONAL RESOURCES

Open educational resource initiatives have increased the options available to help support learning within the classroom. According to the United Nations Education, Scientific, and Cultural Organization (2012), open educational resources are teaching, learning, or research materials that are in the public domain or released with an intellectual property license that allows for free use, adaptation, and distribution. Open educational resources provide a variety of learning content, such as full courses, modules, expert lectures, and much more. The push for creative commons licensing has also led to a wide variety of materials available for open use. Currently, these types of initiatives are popping up all over the place. Here is a short list of places to get you started:

- Creative Commons Search Access (http://search.creativecommons.org): Search services to locate materials with creative commons license for open use.
- MIT OpenCourseware (http://ocw.mit.edu/index.htm): Web-based publication of MIT courses. Includes music courses such as "Introduction to Western Music," "Music Composition," and "Music and Technology."
- *OER Handbook for Educators:* Find robust list of search engines, repositories, open textbooks, and OER projects.
- OER Commons (www.oercommons.org): A network of teaching and learning materials with social bookmarking, tagging, rating, and reviewing. Includes robust search engine for locating specific materials.
- OpenCourseWare Consortium (www.ocwconsortium.org): A free and open digital publication of high-quality university-level educational materials. Includes key word search engine to easily find content.

Given the speed at which new open resources are being developed, consider doing some searching of your own. Many fields have specific open resource initiatives that may help you provide high-quality materials at no cost to your learners. In addition, discipline-specific organizations have rich resources of content to support the course outcomes.

MULTIMEDIA INSTRUCTIONAL MATERIALS

Multimedia can be used to take advantage of the fact that our brains access information in nonlinear ways. The use of different types of media encourages the mind to make connections using text, graphics and illustrations, audio and video, animations, and simulations to make learning concepts more efficient and effective. In addition, it enables learners to choose information in the form that meets their individual learning styles that addresses one of the variables in Rovai's (2003) persistence model. Multimedia can help you provide clarification, elaboration, and explanation of critical concepts in the course, which promotes deep learning. It can also help you model concepts through illustrations and examples and provide practice through interactions and simulations. Given the many responsibilities and tasks associated with creating an online course, you may want to focus on selecting existing media to support the course rather than developing them yourself. However, that depends on your technical skills as well as the institutional support available for the development of custom media pieces for the course. There are many types of multimedia to consider for your online course.

Presentations and Lectures

Presentations and lectures can be a more engaging way to present information and hold learners' attention. In addition, they can highlight important information and concepts that learners need to focus their attention on and provide alternative ways for learners to understand the information presented. There are a number of excellent resources for presentations and lectures on a variety of topics that we will describe later in the chapter. In addition, presentations and lectures can be developed using PowerPoint with or without audio that will enable you to bring in your expertise and personal experience in the field to provide a rich understanding of the information presented in the readings.

Demonstrations

Demonstrations can help learners understand processes, skills, concepts, and other types of information by providing a visual representation. Demonstrations provide learners an opportunity to visually construct an understanding of a concept.

They can be used to help them understand how to solve a problem, reactions that occur in a process, outcomes of an experiment, how to complete a task, steps in a process, and any number of discipline-specific demonstrations of concepts. Because content changes so quickly, we recommend that you do a simple search of your discipline followed by the word demonstration (e.g., physics demonstration) and you will find the most up-to-date list of available demonstrations online.

Virtual Fields Trips

Virtual field trips enable learners to navigate and explore places at a distance. This can provide the learner an experience of being in a place they are learning about, which can be more engaging, and the visual experience can aid in learning. You can search for virtual field trips online and find a number of interesting places for learners to visit. There are many sites that link to virtual fieldtrips that are organized by discipline. Many museums such as the Smithsonian National Museum of Natural History and the National Gallery of Art also offer virtual collections. The Google Cultural Institute offers a diverse set of digital artifacts from around the world.

Once you have found an appropriate field trip, explore the resources available to support learners as they explore the site such as questions for learners to respond to or a scavenger hunt activity, where learners find specific things while on the field trip. If there are no resources available, you can develop your own set of questions that learners need to answer or things they need to find as they explore a virtual site. Remember to map your list of questions back to the course assessments to ensure you are targeting the right experience so learners can demonstrate the course outcomes.

Visual Representations

Creating a mental image is important for comprehension and later recall. One issue with the development of mental images is that most of the ones we create are not accurate, which inhibits comprehension and recall. As you consider important information, concepts, and theories that learners will need to remember, think about how you can provide visual representations of the information to help them create accurate mental images. We described conceptual scaffolding in chapter 7 and the use of knowledge maps and concept mapping tools to create visual images of information for better understanding and recall. If there are concepts that are difficult for learners to understand, consider ways to visually represent information. This can include pictures or slideshows, timelines with important dates, knowledge maps, or other visual representations to help learners make stronger connections with the presented information. You may also want to include tools to help learners create their own visual representations of information as they engage in course materials. For instance, consider study guides to help focus learners' attention on important information in their readings or mapping tools to enable them to organize information as they read for greater recall.

THEORIES AND PRINCIPLES OF MULTIMEDIA

As you consider using multimedia as an instructional resource, it is important to have an understanding of multimedia theories and principles to be able to evaluate multimedia resources. Research has shown us that the brain processes information using two channels — visual and auditory (Mayer, 2001). When information is presented using both channels, the brain can accommodate more new information. If we look at multimedia, auditory narration goes into the verbal system, whereas on-screen images go into the visual system. By taking advantage of this multimodal processing capability and technology-based tools, we can dramatically enhance learning and later recall through multimedia instruction.

Mayer and Moreno (n.d.) describe five major principles that are critical to understanding how to effectively use multimedia to support learning: multiple representation, contiguity, split attention, individual differences, and coherence. Exhibit 8.2 shows the breakdown of each of these principles.

Multiple Representations

The principle of multiple representations relates to dual coding theory. Prompting the use of visual and auditory channels improves comprehension and understanding. Often, learners come into online courses with high expectations that the course will be full of multimedia elements. Many are also accustomed to the lecture-based format of traditional face-to-face courses. Often, a complaint from learners is that the online course is too text based. Using multiple representations can also help address multiple learning styles and help learners with little prior knowledge to create better representations of concepts in their mind.

Exhibit 8.2   Multimedia Design Principles

Principles	Definitions	Examples
Multiple representation	Comprehension is increased through the use of multiple representations of the information; also, may address multiple learning styles.	Text + image Text + animation Animation + narrative
Contiguity	Present text and visual images at the same time rather than separately.	Text + image Illustrations with text embedded or close in proximity
Split attention	Split attention occurs when learners have to split their attention between two different presentations. This can occur when a designer uses a visual along with text. To avoid split attention, use narration rather than a text explanation.	Images or animation + narration
Individual differences	The previous principles are dependent on individual differences of learners, so learners with low prior knowledge benefit most from the principles. In addition, learners with high spatial ability benefit from multimedia more than learners with low spatial abilities.	Low prior knowledge = more representations of to-be-learned material High spatial ability = more multimedia representations
Coherence	Coherence occurs when the information is presented as a concisely as possible without any nonessential details, examples, and distracting media elements.	Exclude unnecessary or tangential examples, stories, or details. Exclude images, sounds, or narration that distract from the concepts being addressed.

Continuity

The principle of continuity focuses on how working memory functions. The information-processing system in the brain is made up of four main components: sensory memory, which receives incoming information; short-term memory, which holds the information; working memory, which processes the information; and long-term memory, which stores information. Working memory refers to the structures and processes used for temporarily storing and managing information in short-term memory (figure 8.1).

Working memory includes the processes by which short-term memory is transferred and stored as long-term memory. It requires organizing complex information before encoding it to long-term memory in order to ensure it is retrievable at a later time. It also includes storing new information with existing knowledge to create stronger mental connections.

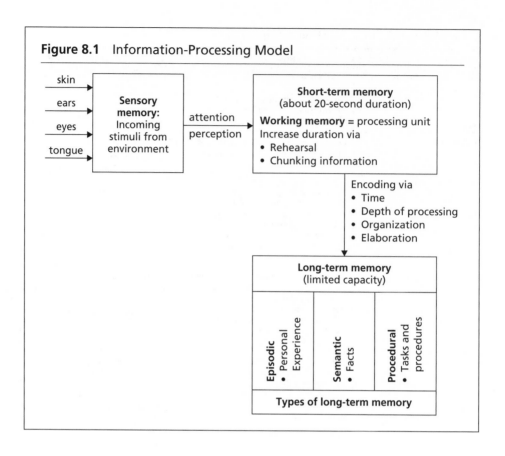

Figure 8.1   Information-Processing Model

There are limits to the amount of information that can be processed at any one time in short-term memory. Research indicates that the number of units or chunks of information that can be processed is seven, plus or minus two (Miller, 1956). The way information is bundled or chunked can have an impact on retention in short-term memory. When considering the use of multimedia, it is important that both words and pictures are located together, so working memory can use all incoming information and make links between them for greater understanding.

Split Attention

Split attention occurs when learners have to split their visual attention between an animation and text, which overloads the visual information-processing system

(Mayer & Moreno, n.d.). Instead, use audio narration, which enables the auditory channel to process the narration and the visual channel to process the animation.

Individual Differences

The principle of individual differences states that the other multimedia principles are dependent on individual differences in prior knowledge and spatial ability. Learners with high prior knowledge are more likely to generate their own mental images, whereas learners with low prior knowledge tend to generate incorrect mental images that negatively affect learning. Learners with high spatial abilities are able to hold the visual image in their working memory longer, which enables them to benefit more from the contiguous presentation of various media.

Coherence

Finally, the coherence principle relates to the idea of presenting just enough relevant information to understand and remember key concepts rather than presenting information with too much detail. This should be a theme throughout your whole course design and can provide a foundation to build and organize additional detailed information after the initial concepts are understood.

These five principles of multimedia design, multiple representation, contiguity, split attention, individual differences, and coherence are important to keep in mind when you design a course. By beginning with a theory of how learners process multimedia information, Mayer and Moreno (n.d.) have been able to conduct focused research that yields some preliminary principles of multimedia design. Their work contributes to the implementation of successful multimedia instruction. Reflecting on these principles will be helpful as you evaluate, select, and create your multimedia to ensure you are supporting learning.

PROCESS FOR SELECTING MEDIA RESOURCES

To begin the selection process, review your course to determine where learners may have the most difficulty with concepts in the course or where visuals and other multimedia may be more effective for learners to comprehend the information. Next, consult with your textbook publisher to see if they have any multimedia associated with the textbook you've chosen. Often, publishers will offer a website that may include lecture slides, images, simulations, and a number of other resources to support the course. Also, connect with your institution for available multimedia that you can repurpose for the course as well as your institution's library to see if they offer any video archives or other multimedia in databases.

There are a number of open resources available that include audio, video, animation, and images:

- iTunes U (www.apple.com/education/itunes-u): Includes lectures, language lessons, and films provided by universities, museums, radio stations, and others

- National Public Radio (www.npr.org): Creates and distributes news, information, and programming about current events, arts, life, and music

- Public Radio International (www.pri.org): Provides unique perspectives on world culture, news, and events

- YouTube (www.youtube.com): Features a wide variety of videos for virtually any topic

- Technology, Entertainment, Design (TED) (www.ted.com): Features videos from individuals with a wide range of expertise and experiences that have a high-quality production value and are available for free

- Learn Out Loud (www.earnoutloud.com): Catalog of audio and video learning including audio books, podcasts, and videos on a wide range of topics

- Podcast Alley (www.podcastalley.com): Features podcast directory and listener-voted top-ten lists

- Khan Academy (https://en.khanacademy.org): Robust self-paced learning tool with videos, exercises, assessments, and progress tracking for math, science, humanities, finance, and other topics

- Multimedia Educational Resource for Learning and Online Teaching (MERLOT) (www.merlot.org/merlot/index.htm): Free and open community of resources designed, reviewed, and created by registered users and faculty development staff; includes online materials, activities, and full course designs; one resource we highly recommend because of the ease of use and ability to navigate easily through content relevant to your subjective matter

- Wikimedia Commons (http://commons.wikimedia.org/wiki/Main_Page): A database of freely usable media files including animations, diagrams, music, speeches, and videos from a variety of fields and content areas

Determine if your institution offers media development services that you can use to produce custom media for the course. Contact your IT department to see if there is any software available for you to use for your online course. Finally, determine if you have time and desire to create your own media. Exhibit 8.3 lists a number of resources and applications available to create multimedia to support the course.

Audio

Audio is an element that can be combined with other media such as illustrations or animation to create a multimedia presentation. Audio may also be used by itself to provide an additional way of presenting information. You may use audio as a supplement or replacement for instructional text, introductions, and descriptions of important concepts, as well as expert stories that help illustrate key concepts as they apply in the field. Just hearing your voice can help motivate learners and can help you develop a greater teaching presence. There are also many applications available that allow you to record your own audio. Audacity is a free, open source software for recording and editing sounds that is available on multiple platforms. Many computers also come with a simple audio recorder such as Sound Recorder on Windows PCs. Many smartphones also have recording devices or applications that can be downloaded to create audio. A quick search for "audio recording" on the web or your preferred application market place (iTunes, Google Play, etc.) will turn up many results. Just be sure to test your audio recording device to make sure the audio comes out clear and you have no audio distractions in the background. Setting aside a quiet area in your home can help ensure clear audio recordings. There are also many guides online that provide additional technical information and tips and tricks for recording audio for the web.

Slide Shows

One way to enhance your audio is through the use of slide shows or screen captures in which you can incorporate images and audio. If you have Microsoft Office, PowerPoint allows you to create slides and add audio recordings to your slides. In some cases, you may also have Adobe Presenter, which allows you

Exhibit 8.3 Multimedia Resources and Applications

Media	Type	Resources
Audio	Audio software	Free open source software: Audacity audio editor and recorder Smartphone recording devices or applications that can be downloaded to your smartphone to create audio
	Audio + visual software	PowerPoint + Adobe Presenter Zentation SlideShare VoiceThread Prezi
Screen capture	Free applications	Jing Screenr
	Commercial applications	Snagit Camtasia Adobe Captivate
	Screen capture software tutorials	Lynda.com
Video	Commercial video capture software	Adobe Premiere Pro Final Cut Pro iMovie Microsoft Movie Maker
	Free software	Animoto Vimeo
Animation	Software applications	Adobe Flash HTML 5 technology Go!Animate Voki
Images	Image creation	Adobe Photoshop Illustrator Microsoft Viseo Inspiration CmapTools SmartDraw Wordle
	Create photo albums of images	Flickr Pinterest

to convert your narrated slides into a web presentation. There are also many applications and software online to help you create or publish slide shows. These include Zentation, SlideShare, VoiceThread, and Prezi. This software can be used with images, diagrams, worked examples, and other visuals to support your narration and take full advantage of the multiple representation principle.

Screen Capture Software

You can also use screen capture software to create slide shows, walk through demonstrations of how to complete a procedure, talk through a paper or image and point out specific characteristics, or even provide feedback on a paper and point out specific areas in which a learner did well or needs improvement. Screen capture software allows you to record all the actions you complete on your computer. For instance, if you want to show learners how to import a file to Photoshop, you could click record and all the movements you make on your desktop are recorded and a file is generated that you may then share with learners. Or, screen capture can be used to introduce learners to the online course environment and how to navigate and use the different tools efficiently and effectively. In most applications, you can also record audio or add text that explains what you are doing. Free applications include Jing and Screenr and commercial software include Snagit, Camtasia, and Adobe Captivate. Commercial sites such as Lynda.com provide many tutorials that include screen capture. Once you've created your screen captures you can uploaded videos to popular sites such as YouTube or iTunesU for easy access.

Video and Animation

Another way to combine images and audio is through video. Video can be used to record yourself talking about a topic and create an experience similar to a lecture, which can enhance your teaching presence. Video requires a bit more advanced technology, although simple technologies such as webcams or smartphone video features can provide an easy way to create videos. There is a lot of commercial software available for video capture and editing such as Adobe Premiere Pro and Final Cut Pro that require more advanced skills but simpler video editing products such as iMovie or Microsoft Movie Maker are also available. There are also some free applications available that help you create video such as Animoto or sites that help you share video such as Vimeo.

Animation

Animation is another option for creating multimedia. Animation incorporates moving images with narration. Often, animations are created by individuals with advanced skills using software such as Adobe Flash or using HTML 5 technology. Easy-to-use and free applications for animation are starting to pop up. Sites such as Go!Animate help you create animated videos and Voki allows you to create an animated speaking avatar for your audio.

Images

Images can also help support learner comprehension of new concepts. There are many options for creating your own images using software such as Adobe Photoshop or Illustrator or options for collecting images online to support your instruction. Sites such as Flickr allow you to create a photo album of images. Pinterest is a great site for saving illustrative images around the web in one place for viewing. Diagrams and concept maps can also help you to create illustrative images for your content. Software such as Microsoft Visio or Inspiration or free applications such as CmapTools and SmartDraw can help you create simple diagrams, flowcharts, and concept maps to help learners better comprehend key concepts. Wordle also provides a great way to illustrate text themes. Wordle allows you to upload text and create an image with words in different sizes to show frequency. This can be used to show key themes in content or even to analyze responses to survey questions. In addition to using these options to create course content for your online course, you can also let learners loose on these tools to create their own products.

EVALUATING INSTRUCTIONAL MATERIALS

As you evaluate course material options, you want to make sure the resources you select are appropriate for your learner population. Learners have preconceived ideas about a field of study and how it fits with their educational and professional goals. They need to be able to see a connection between the course materials and their goals in order to stay motivated and attend to the information presented. Reading skills are also a factor to consider. Many learners may come into the online environment with poorly developed reading skills. Assessing your learners' potential reading level and selecting appropriately leveled materials help to ensure they will be successful with the readings necessary to complete the course.

As you consider your instructional materials, it is important to keep in mind how the resources will help your learners achieve the course learning outcomes and consider the relevancy of the materials to learners' educational goals. Exhibit 8.4 is a resource evaluation checklist to use as you evaluate course materials. As you select instructional resources, use the checklist and go through all of the criteria for the resource. Place a checkmark in the left column to indicate the resource meets the criteria.

Once you have completed the checklist for a resource, evaluate the results. If you find media that do not earn a "yes" answer, you will need to make a decision on the value of the resource because some of the criteria are missing.

COPYRIGHT CLEARANCE FOR COURSE MATERIALS

As you select course materials, it is important to understand copyright in relation to your online course and the resources you use. US copyright grants creators the right to protect and use creative expressions for their own purposes. Copyright policy stipulates that using someone else's work and expression is against the law and can lead to a lawsuit. Violating copyright can damage the reputation of an institution and lead to high financial costs associated with litigation.

Fair Use Act

Education is granted limited exemptions to present copyrighted works to further ideas and foster thought without fear of retribution. Three main acts inform the use of materials by educational institutions. First, the Fair Use Act allows use of copyrighted works for critique, comment, news reporting, teaching, researching, and scholarship. The Fair Use Act set out four factors in the consideration of fair use (US Copyright Office, 2007):

- "The purpose and character of the use, including whether such use is of commercial nature or is for nonprofit educational purposes" supports use for nonprofit purposes more than for for-profit purposes.

Exhibit 8.4 Resource Evaluation Checklist

	Text Resource
	Appropriate to meet the learning outcomes of the course
	Uses the entire book rather than a small portion (if no, then review all content from the source to see if there is an opportunity to create a custom text with the content from the variety of sources)
	Fits within the recommended costs for student learning materials
	Credibility of the author (Who is the author of the information? What are his or her credentials? Is he or she considered an expert in the field?)
	Representative of differing viewpoints (Does the author represent a particular point of view or bias? If so, have you included additional resources to ensure learners get a full understanding of all viewpoints? Does the author cite authorities to support his or her views and conclusions?)
	Appropriate reading level for learners
	Learners have appropriate level of prior knowledge to comprehend the information from the resource.
	Recent copyright date is appropriate to the subject; if more than ten years, then determine if the information presented is foundational and has not changed over the years.
	Media Resource
	Appropriate to meet the learning outcomes of the course
	Fits within the recommended costs for student learning materials or course development budget
	Credibility of the author (Who is the author of the information? What are his or her credentials? Is he or she considered an expert in the field?)
	Representative of differing viewpoints (If applicable, does the media piece represent a particular point of view or bias? If so, have you included additional media sources to ensure learners get a full understanding of all viewpoints? If applicable, does the media piece cite authorities to support his or her views and conclusions?)
	Learners have appropriate level of prior knowledge to comprehend the information presented in the media.
	Recent copyright date is appropriate to the subject; if more than ten years, then determine if the information presented is foundational and has not changed over the years.
	Do the media use multiple representations of the information?
	If applicable, are text and visual images presented at the same time rather than separately?
	If applicable, do the media avoid split attention by using narration rather than a text explanation to go along with a visual image?
	Is information in the media presented as concisely as possible without any nonessential details, examples, and distracting media elements?
	Are the media accessible to all learners or provide a suitable alternative such as transcripts or similar content in another format?

- "The nature of the copyrighted work" supports the use of published factual works and does not cover most use of fictional works.
- "Amount and substantiality of the portion used in relation to the copyrighted work as a whole" supports the use of smaller portions of works.
- "The effect of the use upon the potential market for or value of the copyrighted work" supports a use that does not affect the marketability of work.

Together, these factors indicate that a small portion of a factual work for nonprofit purposes often is allowable, although, for-profit educational institutions may also use fair use materials as long as the other factors are addressed.

TEACH Act and Digital Millennium Copyright Act

The Technology, Education, and Copyright Harmonization (TEACH) Act (2002) provides copyright guidelines and exceptions for distance education. This act expanded copyright to digital works and expanded the definition of education classrooms to include online classrooms. Finally, the Digital Millennium Copyright Act (1998) implemented two World Intellectual Property Organization treaties to make US copyright consistent with world copyright protections. This act limited the liability of online service providers for copyright infringement. It also further refined copyright guidelines for distance education and provided additional provisions unrelated to education.

Some resources are available without seeking permission:

- Government websites
- Website home pages
- Materials owned by the institution's library
- Royalty-free photo databases
- Royalty-free music
- Royalty-free animations

Other Copyright Issues

There are also some specific issues that tend to get us into copyright problems. First, linking to pages past a home page of a website enables your learners to bypass potential log-ins and ads and is considered redistribution of a page. Unless a website provides open permission for this type of link in their copyright statement, you must ask permission to link to the embedded page. Internet articles also pose a potential copyright violation. Although many articles are available online, using them in your course may be considered redistribution. Permission must be procured to use these resources, and in some cases, you may have to pay a fee for use. The Copyright Clearance Center (www.copyright.com) is a great resource for checking copyright fees for specific materials. Another general issue that is difficult for course development is interpreting the copyright notice for websites and online resources. The language is not standardized and can be difficult to interpret. When in doubt, it's good to ask for permission. This is especially true if you work at a for-profit institution. Many copyright statements specify permissions for noncommercial use and do not apply to for-profit institutions.

Using the summary in exhibit 8.5, evaluate the need for copyright clearance of the instructional materials you have selected.

ACCESSIBILITY OF ONLINE COURSE MATERIALS

Accessibility is another important consideration when selecting course materials. If learners are unable to use the course materials because of disability concerns, this poses a significant barrier to persistence. In the United States, Section 508 of the amended Rehabilitation Act of 1973 stipulates that electronic and information technology developed, procured, maintained, or used by federal agencies allows "individuals with disabilities who are members of the public seeking information or services from a Federal department or agency to have access to and use of information and data that is comparable to the access to and use of the information and data by such members of the public who are not individuals with disabilities" (US Congress, 1998b). Section 504 of the act stipulates that programs or activities receiving federal financial assistance must not exclude, deny benefits, or discriminate against individuals solely based on a disability (US Congress, 1998a). If your institution receives federal financial aid, these section 508 regulations apply to your online course.

Exhibit 8.5   Summary of Copyright Law for the Online Environment

Nonprofit Educational Institutions	For-profit Educational Institutions
Section 107 of the Copyright Act of 1976—Fair Use Allows instructors in nonprofit institutions to use works without requiring copyright clearance. In determining whether fair use is appropriate, the following factors should be considered:	
The purpose of the use and whether it is for nonprofit educational purposes: If the purpose is not educational in nature or is being considered in a for-profit educational institution, you will not be able to use fair use as a defense for not receiving copyright clearance.	If you are teaching an online course at a for-profit institution, it is important to understand that fair use does not cover for-profits because the language is specific to nonprofit institutions.
The nature of the work copyrighted: Generally, if the work is fiction or unpublished, or if the work is intended for the educational environment, for example, in the form of a case study or workbook, it will be difficult to use fair use as a defense.	
The portion of the work used: If you are considering a large portion of the original work or a portion of the work that is central to the work, then fair use is not an acceptable defense unless it is being used for a critical analysis.	
The effect the use has on the market or value of the work: If you make the information available to the public, keep it available for a long time, or are planning to make many copies—all of which could replace sales or diminish the market of the copyrighted work—fair use is not an acceptable defense. In addition, if getting copyright clearance is not very costly or timely, you have less of a defense for fair use.	
Section 110(1) of the Copyright Act of 1976 Exemption for nonprofit institutions from copyright infringement when works are used by teachers in the face-to-face classroom:	
Face-to-face: This allows teachers to display or perform works, but does take into consideration making copies of works.	Does not apply to for-profits
Online: It does not allow posting works electronically on a server, which would be the means of displaying or performing works in an online environment, so there is no affordance for educators teaching in an online environment to use works for educational purposes.	
Section 110(2) of the Copyright Act of 1976—TEACH Act The TEACH Act allows online instructors some of the same opportunities as face-to-face instructors. If you are teaching for a nonprofit institution, these three exemptions should be considered as you determine the use of resources in your online course:	
There are limitations to the amount of materials within specific types of works that can be used.	If you are teaching an online course at a for-profit institution, it is important to understand that the TEACH Act does not cover for-profits because the language is specific to nonprofit institutions.
In addition, there are requirements to ensure protection, so only learners in the course have access to the materials and cannot retain copies of the materials or disseminate copies to others.	
In addition, institutions must have copyright policies in place and display them in the course regarding copyrighted materials.	

There is currently a debate in higher education about whether this translates into a requirement to incorporate compliance during the development of online courses or whether accommodations may be made on a case-by-case basis. Typically, institutions have their own interpretations of compliance, often called ADA compliance, and specific policies stipulating accommodation requirements. You may already be familiar with these requirements in your face-to-face courses if you had to make accommodations for your learners such as providing additional time to complete tests. If you are unfamiliar with your institution's policy and interpretation of the legislation, contact your disability services department for additional information and clarification.

The United States General Services Administration also provides tutorials, guidance, and checklists for creating accessible documents in a variety of programs, information about screen readers and what makes websites compliant, along with links to additional government resources related to compliance with section 508. The United States Department of Education also provides a list of requirements for accessible electronic and information technology design that helps you ensure accessibility in the courses. Many of the elements on the list require more advanced IT knowledge to interpret. Exhibit 8.6 shows some of the specific functional requirements for web-based information most applicable to online courses that you should consider. These elements will not ensure accessibility but will help you get closer to incorporating accessible materials in your online course.

Once you have selected all of your instructional materials you should do a final analysis using your instructional materials selection worksheet (exhibit 8.1) to determine if you have selected adequate materials to achieve each of the course outcomes. This analysis will also help you reconsider important information and concepts related to an outcome that you may want to enhance by searching for or creating additional content. You may also find that you have included more resources for some competencies and less for others, so you will want to evaluate whether you need to look for additional resources.

In this chapter we described how to select instructional materials to fulfill your course outcomes. It is important that your instructional materials provide adequate breadth and depth necessary to achieve those goals. In addition, it's important that you use a variety of representations of key information and

Exhibit 8.6 Functional Requirements of Web-Based Information

Specific Functional Requirements	Evaluation Strategies
Web-Based Intranet and Internet Information and Applications	
A text equivalent for every nontext element shall be provided.	If you roll over an image, a text description of the image should show up or there should be an explanation of the image in text form near the image. Audio files should have a text transcript of the content available.
Equivalent alternatives for any multimedia presentation shall be synchronized with the presentation.	Closed captioning should be an option with a video or multimedia presentation often indicated by [add image].
Web pages shall be designed so that all information conveyed with color is also available without color, for example, from context or markup.	Color-coded graphs and images can be understood without color differences or have a text explanation.
Row and column headers shall be identified for data exhibits.	Exhibits should have clearly marked headers that label the information contained in the exhibit.
Pages shall be designed to avoid causing the screen to flicker with a frequency greater than 2 Hz and lower than 55 Hz.	Avoid content pages that include flashing lights or animated images.
A text-only page with equivalent information or functionality shall be provided to make a website comply with the provisions of this part when compliance cannot be accomplished in any other way. The content of the text-only page shall be updated whenever the primary page changes.	If multimedia does not include closed captioning, a text equivalent is provided such as a web page with an explanation or transcript of the media.
When a web page requires that an applet, plug-in, or other application be present on the client system to interpret page content, the page must provide a link to a plug-in or applet that complies with the requirements for the software applications and operating systems.	This element requires more technical knowledge of applets, plug-ins, and other applications to evaluate completely. Avoiding content that requires additional downloads to access the functionality is a simple way to be in compliance.
When electronic forms are designed to be completed online, the form shall allow people using assistive technology to access the information, field elements, and functionality required for completion and submission of the form, including all directions and cues.	A simple indication of this element is if you can use your keyboard and tab through a form to complete it.
When a timed response is required, the user shall be alerted and given sufficient time to indicate more time is required.	A web page doesn't time out when you are reading the content or a pop-up with an indication for more time is provided. In the case of online tests, often there is an option to not make it timed, which can also bring you into compliance.

concepts related to your outcomes to ensure they meet different learning styles and provide learners an opportunity to comprehend and recall information by using all of their senses.

Action Steps

To help you apply the concepts in this chapter, complete the following:

- Review the course learning outcomes and competencies to determine instructional material needs. Use exhibit 8.1 as you begin the process of selecting instructional materials.
- Send your list of course learning outcomes to your publishers to have them help you find appropriate resources that map specifically to the course. If your outcomes map to several textbooks from a publisher, consider creating a custom text. Also, ask the publisher if any of the textbooks you select are scheduled for a major edit that could affect the course design.
- Review your institution's library resources and additional open sources for quality materials to support your learning outcomes and competencies.
- Review your outcomes and competencies to determine where learners may have the most difficulty with concepts in the course or where visuals and other multimedia may be more effective for learners to comprehend the content.
- Review the resources you have chosen using the evaluation information provided in exhibits 8.4 to 8.6 and your completed instructional materials selection (exhibit 8.1) worksheet to ensure the quality of your materials and alignment to the course learning outcomes and competencies. If there are gaps or materials that do not fit the criteria, search for additional existing content or consider creating your own content.

Design of Effective Course Activities

OBJECTIVES

After reviewing this chapter, you should be able to

- Select appropriate instructional activities for your online course based on course learning outcomes and competencies.
- Select active learning strategies that enable learners to move from lower levels of knowledge and comprehension to levels of application, synthesis, evaluation, and creation to achieve course learning outcomes.
- Select instructional strategies that encourage presence in your course and support learners' successful achievement of course learning outcomes.

Once you have selected your instructional materials, you need to design course activities that will transform the information learners have read, listened to, and viewed into knowledge they can use. The instructional activities you choose should enable learners to recall, demonstrate, practice, explore, discover, refine, and perfect their knowledge and skills. Learners will also need to be able to connect what they've learned with how it's applied. Therefore, instructional activities should provide learners' opportunities to apply their knowledge, skills, and understanding in authentic situations and connect discrete knowledge and skills with a deeper understanding of how they work together in actual applications learners will confront in practice. All of the activities you design should support the achievement of the course learning outcomes. When you select your instructional activities, your goal should be to choose activities that enable learners to move from lower levels of knowledge and comprehension to levels of application, synthesis, evaluation, and creation at the higher end of Bloom's taxonomy.

INSTRUCTIONAL STRATEGIES MAPPING

In chapter 8 you mapped your instructional resources to the course outcomes and assessments. When you design your instructional activities, you will also want to ensure the activities you choose align to the course outcomes and competencies and help learners develop appropriate knowledge, skills, and attitudes to perform well on the assessments that will measure the extent to which they have achieved the course outcomes. The instructional strategies mapping worksheet (exhibit 9.1) is a tool to help ensure this alignment. In addition, you should also map the activities to the levels of Bloom's taxonomy to ensure that you design activities that help learners move from the lower end of Bloom's taxonomy (know and comprehend) to higher levels of the taxonomy (synthesize, evaluate, create). Exhibit 9.1 provides an example of some initial instructional strategies ideas for our English 101 example.

Think about activities that enable learners to demonstrate they have read the materials and understand basic concepts and important information. Then consider activities that learners can engage in to turn that information into knowledge including practice activities and collaborative learning strategies. Practice activities should provide learners with opportunities to apply the information they have gained. You will also need to design instructional strategies that ensure learners are able to connect the information and knowledge they gain throughout the course and use them in novel situations that reflect the real world. High-level learning activities should enable learners to ponder complex subjects and issues, develop questioning skills, conduct research, and create projects to name a few options. For instance, you can have learners work with a team on a project in which learners have to apply real-world team strategies, project management, and critical thinking, and integrate skills, knowledge, and attitudes to solve real-world problems.

Exhibit 9.1 Instructional Strategies Mapping Worksheet

Outcomes and Competencies	Assessments	Instructional Strategies		
		Know and Comprehend	Apply and Analyze	Synthesize, Evaluate, and Create
Apply writing process to create effective writing products such as papers and presentations. • Use brainstorming and outlining strategies to initiate writing process. • Locate scholarly and practitioner resources appropriate to audience and writing purpose. • Use drafting and revising strategies to refine writing products (papers and presentations). • Proofread papers and presentations to correct grammar, mechanics, and usage issues.	Final writing products: • Artifacts of writing process, for example, brainstorms, outline, annotated references, drafts • Self-assessment • Quiz • Audience analysis • Annotated bibliography • Outline • Draft paper • Peer review	• Interactive exercise to put the parts of the writing process together in the correct sequence with feedback about why • Discussion about how writing is used in learners' professional fields; include informal brainstorm of writing products for final assignment • Practice exercise to proofread and correct a paragraph of text	• Discussion about one to three resources found to support final writing product; include evaluation of resource • One-on-one tutoring sessions in the writing lab to apply writing process, as necessary	• Reflective discussion about previous writing experiences and strengths and weaknesses related to writing • Checklist to evaluate personal writing process to identify strengths and areas for improvement
Adhere to conventions of standard written English to effectively communicate ideas. • Use appropriate capitalization and punctuation. • Use appropriate sentence structure. • Follow grammar rules including tenses and subject-verb agreement. • Spellcheck work and correct any misspellings.	Final writing products: • Self-assessment • Quiz • Annotated bibliography • Draft paper • Tutor review	• Review and correct errors in a paragraph of text. • Practice exercise to create strong sentence structure • Practice exercise to create effective paragraph structure	• Draft an effective sentence for peer review. • Draft a paragraph of text for peer review. • One-on-one tutoring sessions in the writing lab to apply writing conventions, as necessary	• Reflective discussion about strengths and weaknesses related to writing conventions • Checklist to evaluate writing products to identify strengths and areas for improvement

(continued)

Exhibit 9.1 *(continued)*

Outcomes and Competencies	Assessments	Instructional Strategies		
		Know and Comprehend	Apply and Analyze	Synthesize, Evaluate, and Create
Apply appropriate form and style to clearly and concisely present ideas. • Use appropriate paper structure based on relevant style guide. • Cite references appropriately in text and at the end of the paper in a reference list or bibliography according to a style guide. • Use appropriate headings.	Final writing products: • Self-assessment • Quiz • Format writing sample • Annotated bibliography • Argument analysis worksheet • Tutor review	• Practice exercise to identify form and style errors and correct them • Practice to format a text excerpt using proper in-text citations and references • WebQuest to identify additional resources related to form and style practice	• Annotated bibliography practice discussion for one to two references	• Checklist to evaluate form and style in writing products
Integrate critical thinking strategies to provide logical arguments and adequate support for ideas to persuade target audience. • Practice using a critical thinking model to evaluate and construct arguments. • Develop logical arguments using proper support. • Adapt communication to specific audiences.	Final writing products: • Self-assessment • Quiz • Audience analysis • Annotated bibliography • Research analysis worksheet	• Exercise to explain the different components of a critical thinking model • Exercise to identify critical thinking errors in writing	• Discussion scenario to craft a logical argument to persuade others • Discussion scenarios to analyze and determine appropriate adaptation techniques	• Checklist to evaluate logic in writing products

PRACTICE STRATEGIES

Once learners have completed the reading assignments and viewed all of the instructional materials for a unit of study, it's important to provide them opportunities to demonstrate they have the basic foundational knowledge and understanding to move on to activities that enable them to apply what they've learned. Practice activities enable learners to apply what they are learning and receive formative feedback to clarify, redirect, or confirm understanding. Practice activities should be used prior to activities in which learners will need to use information at the higher levels of Bloom's Taxonomy. These activities can also help learners gain valuable skills they will need in the real world. Horton (2012) recommends that you use practice activities to do the following:

- Prepare learners to apply skills, knowledge, and attitudes in real situations.
- Teach learners to adapt general, abstract knowledge to specific, concrete situations.
- Automate skills and consolidate separate bits of learning so that application is faster and more fluent.
- Build confidence in the ability to apply learning.
- Verify the ability to apply low-level skills or knowledge before moving on to more complex items. (p. 130)

Practice activities should be sequenced from simple to complex to support learning and provide learners with opportunities to gain confidence in their ability to apply basic ideas before they move on to more complex applications and higher levels of understanding. Practice activities are an effective way to help learners develop automaticity in using specific skills and knowledge, meaning they are able to perform without an awareness of their thinking. For instance, when learning to ride a bike, you have to pay attention to balance, steering, and pedaling, which requires the ability to attend to a number of things at the same time. Once you learn to ride a bike, you do not need to exert the same cognitive effort because it has become second nature or automatic. Practice also helps learners in developing critical thinking and problem-solving skills as well as steps in a process or in solving a problem. There are a number of practice activities that learners can engage in online in many disciplines including language learning, anatomy and physiology, and geography to name a few. In math there are a number of practice environments that enable learners to use calculators, graphs, formulas, and an endless array of practice activities online. You can search Merlot.org (www.merlot.org) or do a simple search of "online math practice activities" and you will find a number of resources. Merlot.org enables you to select drill-and-practice activities and then you can search by discipline to find appropriate resources.

Comprehension Strategies

Comprehension strategies provide important information to you and your learners regarding the extent to which they have acquired the foundational knowledge needed before they move on to apply what they've learned. Activities include quizzes, flashcards, puzzles, study questions, as well as a number of other activities to support the lower end of Bloom's Taxonomy.

A quiz is a formative assessment activity that can help ensure learners have read the materials and provide them with an understanding of their current level of comprehension and where they need to focus more time on absorbing important information and understanding important concepts. It also gives the instructor insight into areas where learners may be having difficulty as a whole, which provides an opportunity to use direct instruction to elaborate on concepts learners are struggling with. Most learning management systems (LMSs) have a quiz feature or your publisher may have quizzes built into the online content associated with the textbook you chose for the course. You may want to design your quizzes after you have developed the rest of your instructional activities to ensure you are quizzing learners on important foundational information and concepts they will need to know to progress through the course activities.

Puzzles, flashcards, and study questions can focus learners' attention on important information from the course materials and can be a fun way to practice vocabulary and recall basic facts. Think about the important concepts that are essential for learners to understand in the course and create activities that will demonstrate learners have the foundational knowledge and comprehension to move on to higher levels of thinking. If you do a search of "online puzzle maker," you will find a number of resources to help you create puzzles. The Flashcard Machine (www.flashcardmachine.com) is a great tool to make flashcards or you can have learners to make their own flashcards. Study questions can help learners attend to important information in the readings. You can use fill-in-the-blank and open-ended questions to help learners focus on important concepts.

Once you have created instructional activities that ensure learners have the foundational knowledge and understanding of key concepts and skills, you will need to consider instructional strategies for learners to use the knowledge they have gained. Think about different types of activities that will enable learners to apply and analyze what they've learned.

Virtual Practice Strategies

When you think of instructional strategies that focus on higher levels of Bloom's Taxonomy, consider virtual practice strategies such as simulations, virtual labs, and virtual worlds so learners can experience and practice the use of knowledge, skills, and attitudes as they are used to solve problems in the real world.

Ijsselsteinjn, de Ridder, Freeman, and Avons (as cited in Lehman & Conceição, 2010) describe four modes of presence—realism, immersion, involvement, and suspension of disbelief—that can support higher-order thinking and make the boundaries between the real and virtual environment transparent. *Realism* is a mode of presence that enables the learner to engage in experiences that reflect the real world. It provides learners an opportunity to engage in learning by using their senses of vision, hearing, and touch. *Immersion* creates a sense of presence through the illusion of reality in a virtual environment. Learners are able to navigate an environment, interact with peers, and learn through the simulation of a real-world environment. *Involvement* enables learners to interact with peers via technologies that create a greater sense of real-world understanding of the complexity of interactions that can change outcomes. Finally, *suspension of disbelief* enables learners to create their own reality in their minds even though they are aware that in reality it is not true. This can provide learners with the opportunity to engage in experiences that, even though the characters are not real, offer rich engagement and learning. Regardless of the technology used, "the important aspect of the experience for the learners is to provide a sense of 'being there,' a feeling that they are present in the total learning experience" (Lehman & Conceição, 2010, p. 20).

Simulation

Simulation provides learners an opportunity to engage in an event or situation that closely resembles the real world, providing opportunities for realism and immersion. Students learn better through simulation because they are involved in active learning that requires them to inquire, investigate, and apply knowledge and skills as they take full control of the decision-making process in the simulation. The use of simulation supports the application and integration of knowledge, skills, attitudes, and critical thinking. It encourages learners to "think on their feet" as they engage in the simulation, responding to situations that require them to make decisions along the way that may affect the outcome of the simulated event.

Virtual Lab

For activities that require hands-on experience, consider virtual labs that enable learners to practice skills in a simulated environment in which risk from error is low. You can also use virtual laboratories for discovery and guided practice activities. According to Horton (2012), discovery activities are good for exploratory learning, to reveal principles, and to stimulate curiosity about a subject. Guided practice enables learners to complete steps in a procedure or task with feedback along the way to ensure learners are able to successfully complete one step before moving on to the next. This is important to help learners develop a systematic process for completing a procedure or task and also helps them understand exactly where they go wrong along the way.

There are a number of virtual labs and simulations available. As we mentioned previously, Merlot.org has a number of online instructional activities including virtual labs and simulations by discipline. You can use the search at the top of the page or search by discipline or type of material you are looking for. From a preliminary search of virtual labs we did, we found 25 results and from a search of simulations we found an additional 897 results, so you can see that there are a wide variety of resources. In the field of economics "The Economics Network" at www.economicsnetwork.ac.uk/teaching/simulations has a number of economic simulations that enable learners to understand the outcomes of decisions in a practice environment.

Virtual Worlds

Virtual worlds are simulated real-world environments that enable learners to interact with other learners in a real-world context. Virtual worlds are shared spaces that depict a space visually, usually in 2D or 3D, and interactions occur in real time. They enable users to build objects and add functionality to an object.

Learners inhabit a virtual world via avatars, which is a learner's representation of himself or an alter ego, and interact in the environment by performing roles and activities related to that environment. This can create an opportunity for learners to engage in immersive experiences and can also be used to create a "suspension of belief" depending on the application. Quest Atlantic, Fantage, Reaction Grid, and Second Life are examples of virtual worlds (Manning & Johnson, 2011). The benefit of using virtual worlds is that it enables learners to apply the knowledge and skill they gain from the learning content within a real-world environment. It also provides learners with an opportunity to understand the complexity of the real world as well as how individual differences affect outcomes. The interactive nature of virtual worlds makes this type of tool exceptional for being able to construct meaning and retain new knowledge through the shared ideas of learners.

REFLECTIVE LEARNING

We introduced reflection as an assessment strategy in chapter 5; however, it can also be used as an instructional activity that is not graded. According to Brookfield (1987), reflective learning is an important part of critical thinking. Reflection enables learners to consider where they have been, where they are, and where they want to go. With this knowledge, learners can grow as self-directed, independent learners who are in control of their own learning. Self-reflection is also an important scaffolding tool to support the development of metacognitive strategies that enable learners to develop plans for continual improvement by helping them see areas of growth and areas that need additional attention to improve cognitive development and attain the intended outcomes of the course.

To help learners develop reflection skills, consider designing instructional activities that enable learners to reflect throughout the course. You can create reflection questions at the beginning of the course to help learners reflect on their previous experiences to determine their current level of achievement as well as learning strategies. This will provide them with an opportunity to reflect on areas where they need to focus their attention and effort. Throughout the course, there should be additional opportunities for learners to reflect on how they are doing. This can be accomplished through reflective exercises at the end of each unit of study or at the end of major activities and assignments. The exercises should also be forward looking to identify where learners need to focus more effort and attention. By having learners reflect throughout the course, they have a better opportunity to achieve the intended outcomes.

Blogs are collections of writings from an individual that can be used for reflection activities. Wordpress, Blogger, Edublogs, and Posterous are a few examples of the available blogs (Manning & Johnson, 2011). In addition to these blogs, some LMSs such as Blackboard have a blog tool that you can use to create blogs for your learners. Individual blogs can be set up for your course so learners can post thoughts about the course and reflect on how well they are achieving the course goals, knowledge gained and its relevance, areas that need improvement, how they have improved or changed because of course activities, and future goals.

DISCUSSION FORUM ACTIVITIES

Discussion is an integral part of the online learning environment. According to Brookfield and Preskill (2005), "discussions are ideal for exploring complex ideas and entertaining multiple perspectives" (p. 236). It is through collaboration between learners that higher-order thinking skills can be developed, including critical thinking, creative thinking, and problem solving. Multiple perspectives that present new or different interpretations and explanations of a topic of study can help develop learners' conceptions and inform them of their misconceptions during learning.

When deciding on the type of discussion to use in your online course, try to stay away from questions with a single answer or few answers and no room for interpretation. Such questions leave learners frustrated if they enter the discussion late and find that all of the potential responses have already been posted and there is little to add to the discussions without repeating someone else's ideas. In addition, such questions defeat the purpose of using discussion as a collaborative activity for knowledge building. Instead, consider questions that have a number of different ways they can be answered or questions that are open-ended and have no correct answer. The best type of question should pose a question or issue of interest in the form of a problem statement. The discussion question format should require learners to understand multiple perspectives on the question or issue, and the learners' responses should require them to take a position and discuss the implications of their line of reasoning. Questions should enable learners to integrate their knowledge and comprehension of concepts and apply, analyze, synthesize, and evaluate them in real-world scenarios. Application questions enable the learner to apply course knowledge to solve real-world problems. Analysis questions enable learners to discover relationships between concepts and ideas and compare similarities and differences of ideas. Analysis questions also enable learners to break down information to discover causes, assumptions, motives, and make inferences. Analysis questions can also probe issues or problems and ask learners to discover the root cause. Synthesis discussions enable learners to incorporate information in new ways to plan, design, or solve problems in the real world. Finally, evaluative questions enable the learner to judge, critique, or defend their interpretations of concepts.

As you consider how to use your discussion forums consider a variety of activities that require learners to do different things so they don't become bored and their level of engagement doesn't diminish over time. Exhibit 9.2 lists a variety of discussion forum activities that can add variety and enhance learner motivation. They can also meet the different learning styles of learners and support critical thinking.

How to Use Discussion to Promote Critical Thinking

Discussions are a great place to help learners develop strong critical thinking skills. In chapter 7 we discussed engagement and the importance of creating a community of inquiry (Garrison, Anderson, & Archer, 2001) in your online course, which requires strong critical thinking skills. One model that we have found to be comprehensive and relevant to developing critical thinking skills is the Paul-Elder model of critical thinking (Elder & Paul, 2010). This model presents the concept of critical thinking in everyday language that learners can draw on to improve their thinking in class and in their everyday lives.

Elements of Thinking (Thoughts)

The model considers the "elements of thinking," which include purpose, question, information, inference, assumption, point of view, concepts, and implications. According to Elder and Paul (2010), all reasoning has a purpose and is an attempt to figure something out, answer a question, or solve a problem. Reasoning through a question is based on assumptions that are made from a specific point of view.

Exhibit 9.2   Discussion Forum Activities

Activity	Strategy
Antagonistic arguments	Present two credible but antagonistic arguments. Challenge learners to understand both sides by having them post a response to support one of the arguments. Then, ask learners to reply to others who took the opposite side and refute their arguments.
In the news	Post or link to a recent article related to a course topic. Based on the content of the article, ask learners to do one or more of the following: • Evaluate the source • Evaluate the arguments • Apply a theory • Take on a role • Describe an alternative perspective • Describe follow-up questions they would ask
Write a letter or respond to a letter	Create a relevant scenario and have learners write a letter to someone discussing the situation, potential solutions, and so on. Learners can respond to other learners' letters.
Muddiest point	For each week, include a discussion thread that asks learners to describe the muddiest point in the materials they read. Peers can help one another by providing clarification. Instructors can provide additional insight or clarification based on the interactions.
Debate	Set up a somewhat controversial topic; assign learners a side or let them pick; learners present an initial case and then refute the opposite side's arguments.
Collaborative problem solving	Present a problem or issue relevant to topic; as a full class or in small groups, have learners analyze problem and propose solutions.
Role-play	Form four groups of learners and have them take on one of four activities: critique, defend, apply, summarize. Each group will respond to the discussion based on its assigned activity. Critique group: Learners will look at the information and criticize it based on the following: • Alternative view • Lack of evidence or evidence to the contrary • Reliability or validity of source Defend group: Learners will provide support of the scenario by • Verifying credibility of source • Bringing in additional information to support view Apply group: Learners will demonstrate a direct application of the information (i.e., provide real-world examples). Summarize group: Learners will present a summary of the findings.
Case study	Present a real case and ask learners to analyze, break down, diagnose, solve, examine, interpret, and question.

Information, data, and evidence are used in our reasoning. All reasoning is based on ideas, and inferences are drawn from the information to enable us to come to conclusions, which have implications and consequences. Exhibit 9.3 describes what Elder and Paul refer to as the elements of thought and can help learners

Exhibit 9.3 Paul-Elder Critical Thinking Model—Elements of Thought

Thought Element	What to Consider
Point of view	How am I looking at this situation?
	Is there another way to look at it that I should consider?
	What exactly am I focused on? In addition, how am I seeing it?
	Is my view the only reasonable view?
	What does my point of view ignore?
	Am I considering the way other cultures or groups view this?
	Which viewpoints make the most sense to me given the situation?
	Am I having difficulty looking at this situation from a viewpoint with which I disagree?
	What is the point of view of the author of this story, reading, article?
	Do I study viewpoints that challenge my personal beliefs?
Purpose	What is the purpose of the discussion?
	How does this relate to my purpose?
	What is the scope of my purpose—what is and is not included?
	Is my purpose significant, realistic, and related to the purpose of the discussion?
	Am I focused on my purpose throughout my response?
Question	What is the question I am trying to answer?
	What important questions are embedded in the issue?
	Is there a better way to put the question?
	Is this question clear? Is it complex?
	What kind of question is this? Historical? Scientific? Ethical? Political? Economic?
	What would I have to do to settle this question?
Information	What information do I need to answer this question?
	What data are relevant to this problem?
	Do I need to gather more information?
	Is this information relevant to my purpose or goal?
	On what information am I basing my response?
	What experience can I share that is relevant to the question?
	How do I know this information (data, testimony) is accurate?
	Have I left out any important information that I need to consider?
Interpretation and inferences	What conclusions am I coming to?
	Is my inference logical?
	Are there other conclusions I should consider?
	Did I interpret the data correctly?
	How did I reach that conclusion?
	What am I basing my reasoning on?
	Does my interpretation make sense?
	Does my solution necessarily follow from the data?
	Is there an alternative plausible conclusion?
	Given all the facts, what is the best possible conclusion?

(continued)

Exhibit 9.3 *(continued)*

Thought Element	What to Consider
Concepts	What idea am I using in my thinking? Is this idea causing problems for me or for others?
	I think this is a good theory, but could you explain it more fully?
	What is the main hypothesis I am using in my reasoning?
	Am I using terms that keep with established usage?
	What main distinctions should I draw in reasoning through this problem?
	What idea is the author of the reading(s) using in his or her thinking? Is there a problem with it?
Assumptions	What am I assuming or taking for granted?
	Am I assuming something I should not?
	What assumption is leading me to this conclusion?
	What is . . . (this policy, strategy, explanation) assuming?
	What does the author take for granted?
	What is being presupposed in this theory?
	What are some important assumptions I am making for my argument to be true?
Implications	If I decide to do *x*, what things might happen?
	If I decide not to do *x*, what things might happen?
	What am I implying with my statements?
	What is likely to happen if I do this versus that?
	How significant are the implications of this decision?
	What, if anything, is implied by the facts I am sharing?

develop strong critical thinking skills by focusing their thinking as they construct responses to discussion questions.

Intellectual Standards

Along with the elements of thought, Elder and Paul (2010) have developed a set of intellectual standards that are a great way to help learners understand how to engage with one another in discussions to develop a community of inquiry. So many times learners' responses to one another are "good job" or "I agree." One reason for these types of low-level responses is that they have not been taught how to engage in meaningful dialogue in online discussions. Elder and Paul's standards include clarity, accuracy, precision, relevance, depth, and breadth, which can provide great prompts to help learners engage with one another. Exhibit 9.4 includes questions created by Elder and Paul (2010) to support an inquiry model.

Exhibit 9.4 Intellectual Standards

Clarity questions	Could you elaborate further?
	Could you illustrate what you mean?
	Could you give me an example?
Accuracy questions	How could we check on that?
	How could we find out if that is true?
	How could we verify or test that?
Precision questions	Could you be more specific?
	Could you give me more details?
	Could you be more exact?
Relevance questions	How does that relate to the problem?
	How does that bear on the question?
	How does that help us with the issue?
Depth questions	What factors make this a difficult problem?
	What are some of the complexities of this question?
	What are some of the difficulties we need to deal with?
Breadth questions	Do we need to look at this from another perspective?
	Do we need to consider another point of view?
	Do we need to look at this in other ways?
Logic questions	Does all of this make sense together?
	Does your first paragraph fit in with your last one?
	Does what you say follow from the evidence you use to support your comments?
Significance questions	Is this the most important problem to consider?
	Is this the central idea to focus on?
	Which of these facts are most important?
Fairness questions	Do I have any stake in this issue?
	Am I sympathetically representing the viewpoint of others?

Source: Elder and Paul (2010).

The intellectual standards will help learners engage in more meaningful interactions with one another, which can build greater cognitive presence and result in deeper learning. We recommend that early in the course you set expectations for how learners are to engage in discussions and provide them with a guide to ensure they understand the process. You can develop the guide with the Elder and Paul elements of thought and intellectual standards so learners can refer to it as they engage in course discussions.

Critical Thinking Discussion Scoring Guide

To fully integrate this critical thinking model in your discussion activities, we recommend that you grade discussions based on the learner's ability to use critical thinking rather than as an overall participation grade. A discussion scoring guide will help focus learners on using their critical thinking skills and incorporating Elder and Paul's elements of thought and intellectual standards as they construct their responses and engage with peers in discussions. Be very specific about the minimum amount of times a week learners should participate. To develop a true community of inquiry, consider requiring two to three days a week, preferably spaced out to extend the dialogue. Also include requirements for the amount of engagement with other learners. We recommend requiring them to engage with at least two other learners' discussion posts. Exhibit 9.5 is an example of a grading rubric you may use to evaluate learners' use of critical thinking in online discussions.

You can see that we have used a range of points for each criterion, so you can determine to what extent learners are meeting them and apply points appropriately.

PROBLEM-BASED LEARNING

Problem-based learning activities are a great way to help learners develop an understanding of how the knowledge, skills, and attitudes they are attaining can be used in the real world to solve problems. A well-designed problem-based project should help learners think through ill-defined problems and come up with a solution. This type of activity requires learners to take in information, identify gaps in information, and conduct research to fill gaps, analyze information, consider a variety of solutions, evaluate the solutions, and come up with a single solution to solve the problem. You can see that it hits all levels of Bloom's Taxonomy. The problem should reflect a real problem so learners can gain a true understanding of how the knowledge, skills, and attitudes they are developing in the course will help them perform in practice. You can design them as an individual project, but team projects can add a more realistic dimension to the activity and enable them to experience what it's like to engage in real-world

Exhibit 9.5 Critical Thinking Grading Rubric for Discussions

Criteria	Nonperformance	Basic	Proficient	Distinguished
Applies relevant concepts, theories, or materials to argue or support a point of view and posts initial response to discussion by midweek to extend the dialogue (30 percent)	Does not include a point of view or point of view is not developed (0–15 percent)	Does not use relevant course concepts, theories, or materials to argue or support a point of view (16–21 percent)	Applies some relevant course concepts, theories, or materials to argue or support a point of view; posts initial response to discussion by midweek to extend the dialogue (22–26 percent)	Applies and analyzes most concepts, theories, or materials to argue or support a point of view; posts initial response to discussion by midweek to extend the dialogue (27–30 percent)
Applies relevant information (facts, data, evidence, or real-world examples) to support point of view with implications and consequences of reasoning; relevant information is cited and referenced in APA format (30 percent)	Does not apply relevant information (facts, data, evidence, or real-world examples) to support point of view (0–15 percent)	Applies information (facts, data, evidence, or real-world examples) to support point of view, but lacks relevance and does not address implications of reasoning (16–21 percent)	Applies relevant information (facts, data, evidence, or real-world examples) to support point of view; relevant information is cited and referenced; does not address implications or consequences of reasoning (22–26 percent)	Applies relevant information (facts, data, evidence, or real-world examples) to support point of view; includes a discussion of implications and consequences of reasoning; relevant information is cited and referenced in APA format (27–30 percent)
Collaborates with at least two learners, relating the discussion to relevant course concepts and using at least four intellectual standards to extend the dialogue (30 percent)	Does not collaborate with fellow learners or collaboration is not relevant to discussion (e.g., "I liked what you said" or "I think you did a good job on your post") (0–15 percent)	Collaborates with at least one fellow learner, using at least one intellectual standard to extend the dialogue (16–21 percent)	Collaborates with at least two learners, relating the discussion to relevant course concepts and using two to three intellectual standards to extend the dialogue (22–26 percent)	Collaborates with at least two learners, relating the discussion to relevant course concepts and using at least four intellectual standards to extend the dialogue (27–30 percent)
Applies proper spelling, grammar usage, and mechanics (10 percent)	Has six or more spelling, grammar usage, mechanics errors in discussion post (0–5 percent)	Has four to five spelling, grammar usage, mechanics errors in discussion post (6–7 percent)	Has two to three spelling, grammar usage, mechanics errors in discussion post (8 percent)	Has zero to one spelling, grammar usage, mechanics errors in the discussion post (9–10 percent)

problem-solving scenarios in which there are a number of stakeholders affecting the problem from a number of different perspectives.

According to Savery and Duffy (1995), the instructional principles for problem-based learning are derived from constructivism. Principles include the need to accomplish the following:

- Anchor all learning activities to a larger task or problem.
- Support the learner in developing ownership for the overall problem or task.
- Design it as an authentic task that reflects the complexity of the environment in the real world.
- Give learners ownership of the process used to develop the solution; support and challenge the learner's thinking.
- Encourage testing ideas against alternative views and contexts.
- Provide opportunity for reflection on the content and the process. (pp. 138–141)

Barrows and Kelson (1993) describe core characteristics of problem-based learning, which include the need for learning to be learner centered and occur in small groups under the guidance of a tutor who acts as a facilitator or guide. In addition, problem-based learning activities should take place in the context of an authentic problem to achieve the required knowledge and problem-solving skills.

Problem-based learning provides learners with concrete representations of relevant concepts and ideas situated in real-life experience outside of the classroom. It enables them to critically analyze information and come to conclusions. It also encourages dialogue in a community of inquiry among learners to promote alternative ideas and solutions. This requires learners to use critical thinking and active learning to evaluate the information presented. Problem-based learning focuses learning around a problem, question, issue, case, or project. It requires learners to actively use knowledge from the content domain to complete tasks that require them to solve, resolve, and interpret as they engage in learning activities.

According to Barrows and Kelson (1993), there are six objectives that learners should be able to achieve in a problem-based learning activity:

1. Develop a systematic approach to solving real-life problems, using higher order thinking skills (problem solving, critical thinking, decision making).

2. Acquire an extensive, integrated knowledge base that can be recalled and flexibly applied to other situations.

3. Develop effective self-directed learning skills, identifying what they need to learn, locating and using appropriate resources, applying the information back to the problem, and reflecting on, evaluating, and adjusting their approach for greater efficiency and effectiveness.

4. Develop the attitudes and skills necessary for effective team work with others working on a task or problem.

5. Acquire the life-long habit of approaching a problem with initiative and diligence and a drive to acquire the knowledge and skills needed for an effective resolution.

6. Develop habits of self-reflection and self-evaluation that allow for honest appraisal of strengths and weaknesses and the setting of realistic goals. (p. 2)

For learners to be motivated to engage in problem-based learning activities, the problem should be interesting and relevant and not constrained by being too structured with specific solutions. Consider problems or issues that are ill-structured with the potential of multiple solutions. In addition, problems or issues should be based on problems that practitioners face in their field or issues that are of concern in our real lives. The University of Delaware has a clearinghouse at https://primus.nss.udel.edu/Pbl that has a collection of problem-based scenarios and articles to help instructors use problem-based learning. All of the problems have been peer reviewed by experts in the field of problem-based learning. Each problem scenario includes instructor notes and materials to help instructors use it in a course. The clearinghouse is free; however, you have to sign up to access the database, and it takes approximately a week for your request to be approved. For more details on how to set up problem-based activities please refer to *Effective Online Teaching: Foundations and Strategies for Student Success* (Stavredes, 2011).

WEBQUEST

WebQuest is an inquiry-oriented instructional strategy in which most or all the information that learners work with comes from the web. It provides an opportunity for learners to explore and gather information, analyze it, and present it to others. Generally, a WebQuest activity takes place over several units of study or it can span the entire course.

Learners can develop information literacy skills from WebQuest activities. Information literacy is the ability to find, retrieve, analyze, and use information. Because of the explosion of information on the web, it has become increasingly important for learners to have the skills to evaluate information from the Internet. Learners may have poor online research skills and focus on using basic Internet resources such as *Wikipedia* or About.com. One way to develop learners' information literacy skills is to have them reflect on the quality and stability of the materials they find as they explore the web. As part of the setup of a WebQuest, have learners consider the following questions as they conduct their research:

- When was the information published? If more than ten years, then determine if the information presented is foundational and has not changed over the years.

- Who is the author of the information? What are his or her credentials? Is he or she considered an expert in the field?

- Does the author represent a particular point of view or bias? If so, have you included additional resources to ensure learners get a full understanding from all viewpoints?

- Does the author cite authorities to support his or her views and conclusions?

There is an excellent website dedicated to WebQuests at webquest.org that can help you develop a better understand of how to use WebQuests in your online course. In addition, it contains a number of resources to find, create, and share your WebQuests.

COLLABORATIVE WORKSPACES FOR TEAM ACTIVITIES

A wiki is a collaborative workspace that has the capability of being organized as a collection of linked pages. Wikispaces, PBWorks, and Google Docs are examples of wiki environments (Manning & Johnson, 2011). They provide learners opportunities for involvement with one another to increase presence.

We have tried to design group activities using threaded discussions and found that keeping a number of different threads organized in a discussion forum can be difficult. Collaborating to create and edit documents can be difficult as well. Each time a change is made to a document, a new version has to be uploaded to the discussion, which can create confusion regarding which version of the document is the most recent. A wiki provides more structure and can help learners organize information better with linked pages and navigation menus. Pages can be created for individual tasks and deliverables and can be linked together. In addition, most wikis have navigation bars to access pages on the wiki. Wikis provide a place to post comments, so there is a collaborative feature to each page that enables learners to comment on the information being presented, make recommendations, and share ideas. Learners can also edit documents so all learners have the opportunity to contribute to the deliverables of the project. Because of the asynchronous nature of wikis, learners can engage in the activities according to their own schedule. An additional benefit is that learners can control the space, which can enhance their sense of responsibility.

Wiki Matrix (www.wikimatrix.org) is an excellent site to look at the variety of wikis available and compare wikis based on the features that interest you. It compares general features, hosting features, system requirements, data storage capabilities, security and antispam features, development and support, common features, special features, and media and files, to name a few capabilities. James West and Margaret West (2009) have written a book dedicated to describing how to design wikis for online projects titled *Using Wikis for Online Collaboration*.

Throughout this chapter we have looked at a number of instructional activities to support your instructional strategies. We have discussed ways to design active learning strategies to help create an engaging learning experience. If learners don't feel a connection with you and their peers, it will be difficult for them to persist online, so we have looked at a number of activities that enable you to develop presence with your learners and for them to develop presence with one another. We have also considered a number of activities to match different learning styles to motivate learners and help them persist.

As you considered the different types of instructional activities, we asked you to map them to your outcomes, competencies, and assessments and choose activities that support learning at the different levels of Bloom's Taxonomy (exhibit 4.1). Now that you have completed the selection of your instructional activities, refer to your instructional strategies mapping worksheet (exhibit 9.1) to determine the extent to which the instructional activities you have designed will help learners achieve the course outcomes. If you find there are too many activities at the low end of Bloom's Taxonomy, you will need to consider additional activities at the higher end of the taxonomy. The same is true if you find too many of your activities are mapping to the highest level of the taxonomy; you may want to consider different activities that enable learners to demonstrate competence at the lower end of the taxonomy before moving on to activities at the higher end of the taxonomy.

Action Steps

To help you apply the concepts in this chapter, complete the following:

- Review the course learning outcomes, competencies, and assessments to determine appropriate instructional strategies. Use exhibit 9.1 as you begin the process of selecting instructional strategies.
- Review the questions in the action steps in chapter 7 to ensure you are selecting active instructional strategies that encourage presence and align to different cognitive learning styles.
- Review your completed exhibit 9.1 of instructional strategies to determine if you have adequate strategies for each outcome and competency. If there are gaps, brainstorm additional strategies.

Development of Instruction

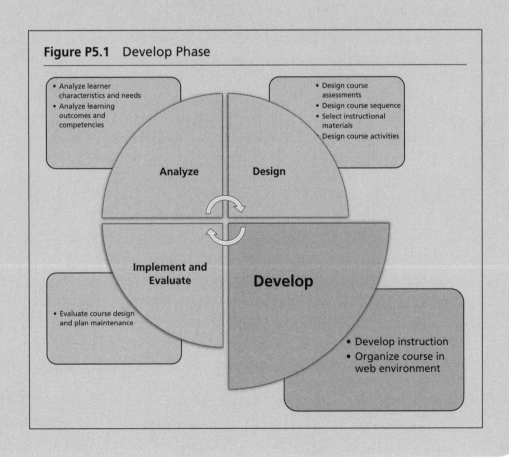

Figure P5.1   Develop Phase

- Analyze learner characteristics and needs
- Analyze learning outcomes and competencies

Analyze

- Design course assessments
- Design course sequence
- Select instructional materials
- Design course activities

Design

Implement and Evaluate

- Evaluate course design and plan maintenance

Develop

- Develop instruction
- Organize course in web environment

Part 5 moves you into the development phase of the course design process when you will organize your content into units of study and then build it out in a web environment such as a learning management system (LMS). In chapter 10, "Development of Instructional Materials," we provide recommendations for how to structure units of study within your course and include a discussion of how to ensure an appropriate balance of work within your course. We also help you develop an introduction to your course and discuss strategies to help clarify and communicate your expectations for learner participation and ideas for helping learners acclimate to the online environment. In chapter 11, "Organizing the Course Environment," we look at how to build your course in a web environment using, for example, an LMS. We discuss important navigation and interface design considerations to ensure that learners are able to easily locate and access course materials and activities and participate within your online course. We also discuss various tools and technologies you may implement to support interaction and facilitate presence in your online course.

Development of Instructional Materials

10

OBJECTIVES

After reviewing this chapter, you should be able to

- Create an organizational structure for the course to develop a consistent learning experience for each unit of study.
- Balance workload associated with course activities in each unit to create a consistent learning experience.
- Write clear and error-free instruction for each of the course components to ensure clear expectations for learners' work throughout your course.

Now that you have chosen your instructional strategies, it's time to work on organizing all of your content into a cohesive course structure to support the achievement of the course outcomes. This chapter helps you determine the types of structure you need to organize your course as well as helps you determine the workload of the course activities and make adjustments to ensure balance among the course units. Finally, you review writing strategies to help you write the instruction for the course.

UNIT STRUCTURE

To begin with, you will need to determine an organizational structure for the course content that will be applied consistently to each unit of study throughout the course. The following components are the most common found in online courses; however, based on your instructional strategies you may include additional elements or eliminate some:

- Objectives
- Introduction
- Readings
- Presentations
- Study activities
- Discussions
- Assignments

Review your assessments and instructional activities to determine which components you would like to include in your unit structure. Then, create a table or alternative format to organize your assessments, instructional materials, and course activities into units based on the sequence you determined in chapter 6.

WORKLOAD

As you organize each unit of study in the course, you need to ensure that you have balanced the workload for learners across the weeks to ensure they don't become overwhelmed in any one unit of study with the amount of work needed to successfully complete the unit. Workload refers to the associated time on task needed to perform each of the course activities in each unit such as readings, activities, and assessments. Many online courses tend toward one side of the spectrum — too many activities and too much workload or the other side of the spectrum — too few activities and not enough workload to justify the credit for the course. Both sides of the spectrum can be detrimental to learner success. Too little workload may lead to boredom and the loss of interest in a course. Too much workload can make learners overwhelmed and frustrated. Keeping the workload relatively similar from unit to unit helps to create a consistent experience for learners and helps them manage their time on task. It also helps you focus your instruction on the most compelling and important content and facilitate learning within your online course. Finally, it helps to ensure adequate translation of the credit workload hours from a face-to-face course to an online course.

Recently, regulatory and accrediting bodies have taken a stronger interest in the definition of student workload associated with credit hours and may be asking for documentation of student workload as a part of the accreditation process. To begin, you will need to know the total hours of instruction for your course. The Carnegie unit is the common means of calculating learner contact hours. It is based on a sixteen-week term and is equal to a minimum of three hours of work per week for a semester. The three hours of work per week includes 1 hour of lecture plus two hours of homework (or three hours of lab), which equates to sixteen hours of lecture and thirty-two hours of homework or forty-eight hours of work over the term per credit. For a three-credit course, you would have 144 hours of workload (48×3). Your program more than likely has calculated contact hours for the curriculum, so you will want to check with someone within the department to ensure you are working with the correct total number of hours of work for your course. You will then divide the total hours over the number of weeks the course will be delivered to get your workload target for each week.

Next, you will need to calculate the time it takes for learners to accomplish the instructional activities of the course. In exhibit 10.1 we have developed a workload worksheet to help you estimate the amount of time dedicated to reading the textbook, reviewing other course materials, assignments, discussions, and other activities, and provided you with some estimates to use in your calculations. We recommend that you build this out in a spreadsheet for the number of weeks of your course, which will also make it easy to build in calculations that automatically add up hours, so you can see the results instantly as you organize activities.

Once you have mapped all of the instructional activities and the time for each activity, review the worksheet and note the units in which you are above or below your target estimate. Keep in mind that one- to three-hour variance between units is a good level of consistency, but you need to make sure the total hours are appropriate for the credit hour of your course. For those units that are off

Exhibit 10.1 Course Workload Worksheet

Activity Type		Week 1		Week 2	
	Estimated Hours	Unit	Activity Total	Unit	Activity Total
Reading or Viewing					
Easy reading (textbook, novel, website, article)—8 min/pg	0.133	no. of pages			
Medium reading (textbook, novel, website, article, etc.)—11 min/pg	0.183	no. of pages			
Hard reading (textbook, novel, website, research article, etc.)—19 min/pg	0.316	no. of pages			
PPT slides—1 min/slide	0.016	no. of slides			
Video—based on length of video. Insert hours directly into "Activity Total"					
Discussions					
Initial posting: 1 hr	1.00				
Reading peer postings: 1 hr	1.00				
Responses to peers: 30 min	0.50				
Other					
Quiz/test: 1.5 min per item	0.025				
Test: 1.5 min per item	0.025				
Paper construction:					
Topic selection: 4 hr					
Outline: 3 hr					
Bibliography: 3 hr					
Draft: 6 hr					
Final: 8 hr					

by more than one to three hours, consider the following questions to increase or decrease the workload:

Too Much Workload

- What are the most important concepts and skills learners need to get out of the course? Are there any important concepts or skills that could be moved to a unit with a lesser workload?

- Which concepts and skills are just nice for learners to know or have? Can you remove some of the materials or activities associated with these elements?

- Are there major overlaps between the textbook and other course materials you have in the unit? Could you make some of those materials supplemental?

- Are there multiple activities that lead learners to the same concepts and skills? Could you remove an activity or decrease the workload for the activity (for example, ten questions instead of twenty) and keep your goals intact? Could you combine activities to get to the same goals while decreasing workload?

- Could you provide learners with additional support for completing activities to reduce the workload such as a template, references for research, or worked examples?

Not Enough Workload

- Have you provided enough time for learners to complete each of the activities? You may want to get a second opinion to confirm your guesstimates.

- Are there additional course materials such as journal articles, websites, videos, or other multimedia that could supplement the content and deepen learners' understanding?

- Could learners use some of the time in the unit for preparing for a future assignment such as researching, drafting, or conducting a peer review?

- Does it make sense for learners to supplement the readings with their own research and review of related content available for the unit?

- Does it make sense to provide learners an additional feedback opportunity in the unit such as a vocabulary quiz, short theme paper, or other activity?

- Could learners go out and experience something related to the content to help deepen their involvement in the topic, for example, a concert or a book reading?

We recommend that you pay close attention to not only the size of the course units, but also to how information is organized to maximize learning.

DEVELOPING UNITS OF INSTRUCTION

Now that you have organized the course content into a cohesive structure and paid close attention to balancing the workload across the units of the course, it's time to develop the individual units of instruction. At the beginning of the chapter we recommended a unit structure that included unit objectives, unit introduction, readings and presentations, study activities, unit discussions, and unit assignments. Following are some recommendations for each of the components of a unit of instruction that help you develop a consistent and effective unit of study.

Unit Objectives

For each unit of instruction, you will need to develop objectives to help learners focus their attention on the most important elements related to competency development and outcome achievement. In chapter 4, you developed outcome statements for the course and associated competencies. Use these statements as the foundation for writing your individual unit objectives. Use the same strategies we described for competencies and learning outcomes to craft objectives that describe what learners should achieve in a particular unit to build toward the course learning outcomes and competencies.

Unit Introduction

For each unit of the course, you should develop a rich description of the unit of study. Your introduction should be used to activate learners' prior knowledge and experience related to new content to help learners make connections to the new material right away. It can also be used to address common misconceptions learners come into the course with or tend to misunderstand when diving into content for the first time. Introductions can also help learners build the knowledge base needed to jump into the readings and activities for the unit.

A unit introduction provides context for the activities learners complete in a unit as well as explain the connections between the activities and the course competencies. These narrative texts are the equivalent of the time you may spend in a face-to-face course introducing a new topic and previewing the activities for the week. Introductions provide an opportunity to explain key objectives for the unit and how the course materials and activities support those objectives as well as any key expectations for performance. They also help facilitate understanding of new content by relating new concepts to be learned to previously learned concepts in past units as well as a broader context in which the content should be viewed such as a field, on-the-job expectations, or a broader topical area. Introductions can also add your personal perspective by enabling you to communicate your own knowledge and skills and add your own insights to the course content. Consider the following questions as your write your introductions:

- What are the most important concepts and skills you want learners to get out of this unit?
- What excites you or engages you about this particular topic?
- How does this unit relate to the overall course learning outcomes?
- How does this unit relate to what learners have already learned — either within this course or previously?
- How does this unit relate to the broader field the topic resides within?
- What are some common misunderstandings that occur when working with these concepts or skills?

Also, consider integrating insights from the course materials required for the unit to help lay the groundwork for learner's completion of readings and multimedia.

Readings and Presentations

This section provides detailed information to the learner regarding the specific readings and presentations associated with the unit of study. If you are assigning readings from a book, include the chapter and page numbers. If you link to a website, make sure that you write specific instructions about what on the website is required to read. You may also want to include a brief introduction for each of the assigned readings to help learners understand the importance of the readings to the overall unit objectives. If you include a presentation, provide a brief overview of the presentation. In addition, include an estimate of how much time the presentation will take learners to go through so they can ensure they have the appropriate amount of time available when they begin the presentation.

Study Activities

You also need to develop your study activity section with introductions to the activities and instructions for completing them. The following questions are meant to help you consider the overall elements to include in those instructions. You may need to add other elements, as necessary, for the particular learning strategy you are using.

- What is a short, descriptive way to refer to this activity?
- What is the goal and purpose of the activity?
- How does the activity relate to the course learning outcomes?
- What are your expectations for learners' participation and the product of their work in the activity?
- Are there specific steps learners should complete?
- What readings, references, and technologies should learners use?
- Should learners collaborate with others?
- If learners need to collaborate or work together, how do you want learners to interact? How many learners will they interact with? How often?

One of the issues we have found is that learners skip many of the ungraded activities and focus only on what they will be graded on. As you review your activities, try to align them with graded assignments to ensure learners complete them.

Unit Discussions

In order to get learners to participate in discussions, we recommend you grade them. In chapter 9, we describe a grading rubric to consider for your discussion activities that focuses on developing learners' critical thinking skills. As you develop instructions for discussions, make sure that you include an introduction to your discussions at the beginning of your course and describe the overall expectations and how they will be graded. If you adopt a critical thinking grading rubric, describe in detail what your expectations are for critical thinking. This is a good time to develop your critical thinking guidelines that we recommended from the Paul-Elder model of critical thinking in chapter 9. For discussions in each of the units of the course, consider the following questions as you develop your instructions:

- What readings are related to the discussion questions?
- What expectations do you have for when learners post their responses to the discussion?
- What expectations do you have for engagement with other learners? How often? What is minimum number of learner interactions?
- How will you grade the activity?

Unit Assignments

Assignment instructions should be rich and detailed to ensure learners have all of the information they will need to successfully complete an assignment:

- A descriptive title for your assignment for example, "Song Composition" or "Historical Analysis"
- An introductory sentence that provides an overview of what you want them to do
- An explanation of the purpose of the assignment
- Details about what the completed assignment should look like
- Details about how learners should complete the assignment
- Information about how you will grade the assignment

The instructions for assignments are often misunderstood by learners because they don't include enough detail, so the learner ends up guessing at what is needed to complete an activity. Include as many details and be as specific as possible with your assignment instructions to prevent confusion and misunderstanding of expectations. It also ensures accurate work and appropriate time on task for learners. It will enable learners to focus on the intellectual work associated with assignments such as critiquing a piece of music or creating a marketing campaign rather than interpreting what they are supposed to do. It can also save you time by not having to return assignments because learners did not follow directions. Consider the following questions as you develop your assignment instructions:

- What is a short, descriptive way to refer to this assignment?
- Why are you giving learners this assignment?
  - What is the purpose?
  - What will learners learn?
  - How is the assignment connected to the course competencies?
  - How is the assignment connected to the purpose of the unit?
- How should learners complete the assignment? What should they spend their time on?
  - If it is a written assignment, what is the expected length? Is that double-spaced or single spaced?
  - What readings, references, and technologies should they use?
  - Are there specific steps learners should complete? If yes, consider developing a worksheet to help them think through each of the steps.
  - Do you want learners to reflect on their outcome or end product and explain what they did to get there? (Reflection can help ensure learners used the correct inputs and processes to complete their assignment and provides you additional cues for evaluation.)
- What should the completed assignment look like?
  - Who is the audience—academics, people in the field, general population?
  - What skills and knowledge should learners demonstrate? Explain fuzzy terms such as *compare*, *evaluate*, and *discuss*.
  - What should be included in the completed assignment?

- How should learners format the completed assignment?
- Can I create a template to help them focus their attention on the right information for the assignment?

As we described in chapter 7, conceptual scaffolding is an important tool to guide learners about what to consider when they are learning (Hannafin, Land, & Oliver, 1999). As you consider your instructions for assignments, think about ways you can help scaffold the assignments to ensure learners know what to consider and can work independently and accurately. Any time you can provide more clarity to the learners regarding the expectations, the more likely they will complete it to your expectations. For every assignment, ask yourself if there is a worksheet or template you can develop to ensure that learners have enough clarity to effectively work through the assignment. Worksheets can be a valuable scaffolding tool to help learners think through important information and focus their attention. For instance, you can develop worksheets for writing assignments to help learners step through the research process, analyze different opinions, respond to particular requirements of the assignment, or a number of other steps, processes, or requirements that learners will need to do to accomplish the writing assignment. A writing template with information on how to construct the different components of a paper can support learners' writing. Your instruction can be written using professional formatting standards such as MLA or APA, which can demonstrate to learners how to correctly set up headings, use citations, and develop a reference list.

Assignment Scoring Guides

Another important part of ensuring learners understand how to complete assignments is to use a scoring guide that clearly outlines how you will evaluate learners' work. This helps to further clarify your expectations for the assignment and provides learners with a tool to ensure their work meets your expectations. It can also provide a way for you to consistently grade learner assignments to ensure fairness across all learners.

There are many different types of scoring guides. In some circumstances, a checklist of specific elements you are looking for provides sufficient information for you to determine the quality of learners' work. In other cases, a more descriptive rubric is necessary to provide distinctions between the level at which learners have achieved different elements. Yet other times, a more holistic rubric is appropriate in which you provide an overall description of what an assignment looks like if learners meet certain levels of performance. At the end of day, it doesn't matter what format your scoring rubric takes as long as you provide learners sufficient understanding of how you are going to evaluate their work and what the distinctions are between levels of performance.

Scoring guides should be based on the competencies learners are supposed to demonstrate in the assignments. The following steps will guide you through the process of developing a scoring guide for the course assessments.

1. Review the alignment of your assessment with the course outcomes. If you have not already done so, determine which specific elements of the outcomes and related competencies learners should be demonstrating.

2. Think about what that performance would look like in the assessment. Take note of the elements learners need to include in their assignment and how they relate to the competencies you would like them to demonstrate.

3. Similar to when you created your specific, measurable competencies, draft specific, measurable statements that capture the elements and how they enable learners to demonstrate the competencies.

4. Determine whether a paragraph that explains all of the elements holistically makes more sense or if it makes more sense to create separate statements. Separate statements are often more helpful because it helps you distinguish between when learners do a good job of demonstrating their competence and when they may be lacking.

5. Determine how many levels you would like to distinguish between. If you just want to have two levels, you may be able to use a checklist with a simple distinction of yes or no or demonstrated or not demonstrated. Exhibit 10.2 is an example of a checklist that could be used for a draft paper in which you are not grading the quality of the paper until learners submit a final draft. For the draft, you can score the paper based on the extent to which learners have included the required components for the paper.

Exhibit 10.2 Example of Checklist Scoring Guide

Criterion	Yes	No	Comments
Includes an introductory paragraph			
Includes at least three sections in the body of the paper			
Includes APA-formatted headings for all sections of the paper			
Includes APA-formatted citations			
Includes a summary paragraph after the body of the paper			
Includes an APA-formatted reference list			

In most cases, you will probably want to have three or more levels. From there, you may decide if you just want to have a general description of what each of these levels entails or specific descriptions for each of the criterion. For instance, you may use the following definitions:

- *NP = nonperforming:* Individual does not demonstrate criterion or demonstrates major misunderstandings related to the criterion.

- *B = basic:* Individual demonstrates foundational elements related to criterion but may demonstrate minor misunderstandings related to the criterion.

- *P = proficient:* Individual demonstrates necessary aspects of the criterion and does not demonstrate misunderstandings related to the criterion.

This type of distinction is easier to write but may leave learners wondering what specifically you are looking for with each criterion. Another option is to create descriptions for each level of your criteria. This would entail defining what each of those levels means for each particular criterion. The following steps can be used to develop the criteria:

1. Think about all the elements and competency demonstration related to a criterion you would like to see to give a learner full credit for the criterion. Use those notes as input to your top level.

2. Think about the common misconceptions, mistakes, shortcuts, and other tendencies you would see in learners' assignments that would take them down a level from that full credit. Use those notes as input to your next level.

3. Continue that process until you have descriptions for the number of levels you would like for your criterion. Exhibit 10.3 is an example of a completed, descriptive scoring guide.

Exhibit 10.3   Example of Descriptive Scoring Guide

Criterion	Nonperforming	Basic	Proficient
Apply writing process to create effective writing products such as papers and presentations.	Applies two or less phases of the writing process such as brainstorming, outlining, drafting, revising, and proofreading; does not provide evidence of continual improvement and refinement of ideas and writing products	Applies three to four phases of the writing process such as brainstorming, outlining, drafting, revising, and proofreading; provides little evidence of continual improvement and refinement of ideas and writing products	Applies comprehensive writing process including brainstorming, outlining, drafting, revising, and proofreading phases and strategies to create effective writing products; provides evidence of continual improvement and refinement of ideas and writing products
Adhere to conventions of standard written English to effectively communicate ideas.	Adheres to few grammar, mechanics, and usage conventions of standard written English to effectively communicate ideas; includes many minor and major errors that distract from the content of the writing	Adheres to main grammar, mechanics, and usage conventions of standard written English to effectively communicate ideas; may include many minor errors and a few major errors that may distract from the content of the writing	Adheres to grammar, mechanics, and usage conventions of standard written English to effectively communicate ideas; may include minor errors that do not distract from the content of the writing
Apply appropriate form and style to clearly and concisely present ideas.	Applies few appropriate form and style elements such as paper structure, references, in-text citations, and headings	Applies some appropriate form and style elements such as paper structure, references, in-text citations, and headings	Applies appropriate form and style including paper structure, references, in-text citations, and headings to clearly and concisely present ideas
Integrate critical thinking strategies to provide logical arguments and adequate support for ideas to persuade target audience.	Creates few logical arguments and inadequate support for ideas	Creates logical arguments and adequate support for ideas to persuade target audience but does not integrate critical thinking strategies	Integrates critical thinking strategies to provide logical arguments and adequate support for ideas to persuade target audience

There are many tools online that help you to develop scoring guides. Some of the more popular online tools are Rubistar and Rubrix. These tools walk you through this process of creating criteria and leveling and provide you a quick and easy way to construct basic rubrics.

WRITING A COURSE INTRODUCTION

Once you have organized the course content into units of study, you will need to go back to the beginning of the course and develop an introduction. In the first unit of the course, you will also want to provide additional activities to help learners acclimate to the new learning environment. This includes providing time for learners to orient themselves to the navigation of the online course and tools and expectations for the skills Rovai (2003) mentions in his model that are essential for online learning: computer literacy, information literacy, time management, reading and writing, and computer-based interaction.

One of the biggest persistence factors influencing a learner's ability to successfully engage in online learning is the clarity of expectations on how to do so. If learners are unsure of your expectations or are just plain confused about how to engage in your online course, it can create early anxiety and result in learners not participating fully and eventually dropping out. In the first unit of the course, it is important that learners feel confident in their ability to engage in your course, so as soon as they link to the course, their focus should clear. In chapter 7, we introduced the concept of cognitive scaffolding to support learner persistence. Procedural scaffolding guides learners as they learn how to navigate the online course environment and engage in learning activities. Learners may have difficulty understanding where to start in an online course especially given the diversity of how content may be delivered online, the variety of resources available, and new expectations for participating in an online course.

An orientation can help learners navigate the online learning environment and provide important information to make them feel comfortable. Palloff and Pratt (2003) suggest the inclusion of Internet basics, basic computer skills, strategies for success, such as time management, an explanation of the role of interaction, how to provide feedback, the rules of netiquette, and support contacts in an orientation. These suggestions incorporate many of the learner skills that Rovai (2003) includes in his persistence model to be successful in the online environment.

You can place a document on the homepage of the course and title it "Start here first" so learners can immediately discover important procedural information to help them begin your online course. You may also consider developing a faculty expectations statement to ensure they are aware of your personal teaching style, the organization and pace of the course, important due dates, and specific policies as they apply to the online setting. Another way to help orient your learners is to develop a one-page course roadmap that lays out the entire course including major topics, readings, discussions, and assignments by the week. This can help learners see where they may need to put in additional time and effort. It can also provide them with an opportunity to plan ahead if they have to travel or need to be out of the course for a few days or a week and can quickly see what they will miss and have to make up.

If learners are primarily online or offsite, you become their gateway to your institution and can help triage numerous issues for learners. Having that support information available can help minimize learner anxiety by enabling them to quickly retrieve critical information to help them just in time. The course introduction should specifically describe the institutional support available to help learners if they have issues. Also, describe technical requirements for your online course such as the best browser to use and any configurations learners need to complete to ensure they receive all content such as enabling pop-ups or accepting cookies and include contact information for technical support. You will also want to provide contact information for key support areas such as administration, learning centers, registration, advising, tutoring, and financial aid. This type of information is so important that you may want to include a link to it in your navigation bar or course menu.

Writing an Introduction to Course Outcomes

At the beginning of the course you should introduce the course outcomes and activate learners' preexisting knowledge and experience related to the course outcomes and associated competencies. As we discussed in chapter 7 when we introduced some foundations of learning, the more you can activate and connect new learning to learners' previous experiences, knowledge, skills, and attitudes, the better they will be able to construct new meanings and integrate them with their previous knowledge. Providing early connections to learners' goals and motivations for pursuing their education helps reinforce what Tinto (1975) refers to as *goal commitment*.

Creating Opportunities for Personal Introductions

Another important consideration is developing social presence (Garrison, Anderson, & Archer, 2001). A critical component of social presence is helping learners create their personal identity in the course. It also is important to create an environment in which learners feel a sense of trust between peers and the instructor. This will enable them to freely engage in discussions and express their thoughts and ideas without fear of being criticized or treated unfairly or with bias. During the first week of the course facilitate a discussion that enables learners to get to know one another. Many learners do not feel comfortable sharing pictures of themselves, so you may want to include as part of an introductory discussion an opportunity to share a cartoon or other image that displays a feeling or characteristic that best describes the learner. Other ideas for introductory discussions are asking learners to share their professional and personal goals, as well as anything personal they would like the instructor and peers to know about them.

You may also want to provide a general discussion thread for social conversation throughout the course to create an opportunity for learners to continue to get to know one another and reach out to one another if they need support. You can post to this discussion area and encourage learners to share favorite places they like to vacation, thoughts on interesting movies, or other topics that construct opportunities to engage in social interactions. This type of discussion can help learners establish themselves socially with you and develop stronger trusting relationships.

You can establish teacher presence at the beginning of the course by creating an introduction to yourself that helps learners get to know you. Share information about your education, professional journey, as well as interesting things that learners may find they have in common with you such as your hobbies, favorite books, or favorite vacation spots. Creating a video introduction or an audio introduction with a still picture can provide an even greater presence. It's interesting how well learners respond to the sound of an instructor's voice. If you can inflect a feeling of sincerity, empathy, and authority, it can help learners sense your concern about and commitment to their success.

Developing Orientations to Processes and Guides

There may be a number of processes or guides that learners will need to follow throughout the course. If the course requires learners to research and write papers, you can include instructions on the process they should use to perform basic research and compose papers. If your institution has research and writing resources, include links to these resources or develop your own resources to support learners' research and writing skills. If you have implemented the critical thinking recommendations from chapter 9, the course introduction should discuss your expectations for developing critical thinking and include a guide to the critical thinking model you will be using along with the scoring guide for discussions, if you have decided to use that for your discussions.

COURSE SYLLABUS

One of the final things you will do is develop a syllabus for your course. Most institutions have specific requirements for syllabi, so we are not going to go into detail on how to create the course syllabus. The important thing to keep in mind with the course syllabus is that it is a contract with the learner and if the learner transfers to another school and wishes to receive credit for the course, your syllabus will need to have enough detail for the new institution to make a decision whether or not to grant credit. Therefore, it is important to list the course outcomes, all prerequisite knowledge or previous coursework required, the textbook and other resources you will be using in the course, an outline of the course topics, and activities, along with major assessments.

GENERAL WRITING RULES

No matter what type of instruction you are writing for your course, there are some simple conventions to keep in mind when writing for the web:

- *Write clearly and concisely.* Individuals tend to skim when reading online so omit needless words and make sure important information stands out by using underlines or highlights.

- *Omit needless words; make useful content more prominent; use shorter pages and noise reduction.* Use short, clear, present tense, and active sentences to portray information easily and keep learners' attention. This will also help ensure learners understand what you are writing because you are not using jargon that learners may not yet be familiar with. If you do use potentially unfamiliar terms, acronyms, and jargon, be sure to define the terms or spell out the acronyms to ensure learners understand the content. Also, be sure to use terms and language consistently to make sure learners can follow your ideas. If you use multiple terms for a single meaning or use the same terms with different meaning, learners may get confused and miss out on your ideas or quit paying attention to the content.

- *Personalization principle.* Use a conversational style and write like you would speak to your learners. The instructional language in your online course is replacing much of the descriptions you would provide verbally in your face-to-face course. To help connect the instruction to both your personal voice and your learners, you need to engage them in the text and not be afraid to bring in your personality. Your instruction should not read like an academic textbook — it should feel more like a conversation between you and your learners. If you are new to online communication media, this may be difficult to begin. One technique is to use a voice recorder and then translate the audio into writing. Or you may want to provide learners instruction via multimedia.

- *Use headings.* It is also important to use headings to break up longer paragraphs for easy reading. This helps learners understand the structure of the information you are portraying as well as signal transitions in content. Bullet and numbered lists also can be used to focus attention on important sections of the text and illustrate relationships among ideas. If the order of a list is important, such as steps in a process, use numbered lists rather than bullets. It is good practice to use bullets or numbers any time you list content rather than serial commas to help learners read and refer back to the information more easily.

- *Use readable font.* The font you use can also help the readability of the course. Sans serif fonts such as Ariel, Calibri, or Verdana are easier to read on screen than serif fonts such as Times New Roman. Also, use 10- to 12-point font, which is the average size for easy reading. Keep your font type and size consistent to remove any potential distraction or barriers. Learners may wonder why you are using different fonts or sizes and if they are missing something. They may also be turned off by the course if it does not look professional. Online learners often interact with many web presences and could not like it if your course is not the caliber of sites they typically interact with.

Once you have developed your instruction, be sure to read your content aloud and review for voice and flow. This will help determine if your personality is coming through in the text and if it adds a human element to the course. It can also help you check for awkward or overly complex wording. Also, be sure to check for spelling and grammar errors. Similar to course materials, what you do in your online course provides a model for your learners. If your instruction is full of spelling and grammar errors, learners may not only question the quality of your course but they also may think that those types of errors are acceptable for their own work. You may also want to have another person read through your work. By the time you get to this point in developing your course, you have looked at similar content for quite a while. Getting a fresh perspective on your course can help confirm that your instruction is clear to your learners and free of errors.

In this chapter, we discussed strategies for creating an organizational structure for the course, balancing the workload associated with the course activities across units, creating individual units of instruction, and developing a course overview. It will take significant time and several revisions to ensure you have a consistent learning experience. This includes clearly explaining your expectations for learner participation in the course activities, making connections among the course elements to form a coherent course, and ensuring the purpose and relevance of the course activities by mapping them back to the course outcomes. Once you have a draft of these components, you are ready to move on to building your course. In the next chapter, we discuss how to build your course in your institution's LMS to support learners' engagement online.

Action Steps

To apply the concepts in this chapter, complete the following:

- Review the course components to determine the parts you need to organize the course. Organize the course assessments, materials, and activities within your unit structure.
- Use exhibit 10.1 to determine the workload of the course activities. Based on your initial analysis, make adjustments to create a consistent amount of workload from unit to unit in the course.
- Write the instruction for each of the course components using the writing rules and suggestions in the chapter.
- Create scoring guides for your assignments and additional cognitive scaffolding, as necessary, to support learners' completion of course assessments and activities.
- Read through your content aloud and review for voice and flow. Make any adjustments necessary to create clear and error-free instruction.

11

Organizing the Course Environment

OBJECTIVES

After reviewing this chapter, you should be able to

- Create a clear interface design within your web environment to help learners easily navigate the course environment and use applicable tools.
- Integrate communication tools to engage learners and support their persistence within the course.

Because information is so readily available in many forms, Internet users have become scanners. We click through sites and make a decision to move onto another page or stay on a particular page very quickly. We also make a fast decision about the quality of a website, so any roadblocks in our way to content can be detrimental to persistence. In web navigation, we quickly move from one site to another until we can easily find the information we need. This directly relates to online learning in at least two ways. First, if learners cannot easily find the information they need, they can become frustrated, which is a barrier to persistence. Second, depending on how you organize content for the web or within your learning management system (LMS), learners may skip important information, which can have a negative impact on their ability to successfully complete course activities.

You may be thinking that navigation and interface design is not relevant for you because you are using an LMS and the navigation and interface has already been designed. However, many institutions give faculty administrative rights to the LMS, which provides you with an opportunity to select from a variety of menu options, tools, and navigation structures. In this chapter, we will discuss design principles that will influence the decisions you make as you select the options available in your LMS or on the web to support your online course.

NAVIGATION AND INTERFACE DESIGN

In the context of online learning, the term *user interface* refers to how you and your learners interact within your online course. Interface encompasses the layout, navigation, and any graphical interfaces of your course environment. An effective and efficient interface for your online course will help ensure that learners are focused on the content of the course rather than figuring out how to navigate the course environment to find information. Some basic design principles can help you effectively organize your web environment or LMS to help learners intuitively navigate and easily use the tools in your course. This ensures that the technology you use does not become a barrier to learners' persistence and success.

Adream Blair-Early and Mike Zender (2008) describe some basic design principles including obvious start, clear reverse, consistent logic, observe conventions, landmarks, and proximity that can help you think through how you use the online environment to organize your course content. Review these principles to ensure learners can effectively navigate the online environment.

Obvious Start

It is important that learners know where to begin when they enter the course for the first time and each time thereafter. We have already discussed a basic strategy of including front and center on the homepage of the course a link to a document titled "Start here first." To make it stand out even more, you may want to use a colored text that is bolded with a different font size from the surrounding text. Each time learners enter the course after the first day, they also need to have a clear understanding how to begin work. Although most LMSs have a navigation bar on the left side of the course, there are choices you can make about what content is included in the menu and how it is labeled. To provide an obvious start for learners each week, include a link on the navigation menu to the unit studies.

Clear Reverse

Many online learners experience the feeling of being lost. This is especially the case if you embed information in different levels within pages of your course environment and the learner has to click through the levels to get to content. It can also be the case if you link to outside resources on the Internet that take them through a series of linked pages. Therefore, it is critical to have a clear reverse and an opportunity to exit or stop when learners want to end what they are doing. When linking to outside sources, have it open in a new window, so the learner simply has to close the window to return to the course. It may not be intuitive for the learner to simply close the window, so you should call this design feature out to them before they click on the linked material. If you are designing interactive activities, the activities should also have a clear exit that allows the learner to leave the activity as well as to start back up at a later time.

Also consider how deep you embed information and have a clear way to navigate deeper into content as well as to return to previous content. Breadcrumbs or links at the top of each page to show previously viewed pages can help the learner to link quickly back to information. Headings for breadcrumbs should be very descriptive to help learners quickly identify the content page they are looking for. Also remember to include an orientation to the breadcrumbs at the beginning of the course, so learners understand how to use them.

Consistent Logic

There should be a logical pattern of relationships between user actions and effects (Blair-Early & Zender, 2008). For example, if there are several locations in the course where learners can upload documents, how they go about attaching and upload documents should be consistent. If you are using an LMS, this type of logic is already built into its design, so you do not need to address this issue. Also consider how you design each unit of study. There should be a consistent presentation pattern for every unit, so learners can become comfortable and develop patterns for approaching the learning activities each week.

Observe Conventions

There are many aspects of design that have become standard practice on the web. Using these practices helps to create a course experience that is similar to learners' other experiences on the web. This includes using a left-hand navigation that follows learners from page to page, using the convention of underlined text in a different color to indicate in-text links, and using elements that look like buttons to submit forms and assignments. It's also important to consider cultural differences when using icons and other interface design elements. For instance, if you use an icon for a navigation element, make sure that it is globally familiar. If not, then also include a word or phrase to ensure learners understand the navigation element. Again, many of these conventions will be built into your LMS.

Landmarks

Often, learners can get lost in an online course because the landmarks are not clear enough to help them locate important information. Landmarks support the user's cognitive map, and help users identify where they are and where they can go in relation to the other aspects of the content (Blair-Early & Zender, 2008). For instance, in the online environment, there are tools and content areas that are very similar for all online courses including a mail feature, discussion room, learning content, assignment submission box, and grade book. These features should be located so they are visible no matter where learners are in the course. Consider this in the construction of your left navigation menu if you have the option to customize it.

Proximity

Consider the relationship between the elements of the course and group-related items together. Elements that are specific to a unit of study should be grouped together for ease of use. If elements will be reused throughout the course, include a place in the course where learners can easily navigate to and search for what they are looking for. Also, learners should be able to navigate easily between course content and tools. Therefore, try not to bury different elements of the course deep within links. This makes it difficult to remember and it also takes a number of clicks to get to the content.

CONTENT DESIGN TO SUPPORT ENGAGEMENT

How you design and organize the content in your online environment can have a big impact on learning. The online environment is very heavy in text. This makes it very easy for learners to begin skipping through information instead of reading completely through it. The way you present information should visually engage learners and help them organize the information being presented.

An interface that fails to engage and keep a user's attention has failed by definition: the user has disengaged and no longer interfaces with the object or content (Blair-Early & Zender, 2008). Consider the use of tables, concept maps, and other visual images to display information that will make it easy for learners to understand the relationship between the information presented. Just as headings are useful in textbooks and papers, course content should be designed with appropriate headings. Related to consistent logic, using consistent headings from one unit to the next can help orient the learner to important information in each unit.

In addition to those principles, Krug (2006) also mentions the importance of eliminating distractions. Similar to the media principles we discussed in chapter 8, it is important to eliminate elements that are not necessary for successful completion of the course. This includes images with little instructional value, background music, and even words. The more concisely you can phrase something, the more likely it is that learners will read your text. If you are not using specific built-in tools from the LMS in the course, you should hide them to minimize distractions. Overall, Krug tells us that we (designers) should do everything we can to get out of the users' way and don't make them think their way through the site. This rule enables users to concentrate on content rather than the form of the website. For more information, check out Krug's website www.sensible.com. Using these principles as you design your online course will help you further support your learners' persistence and success in your course by creating an environment that is intuitive and keeps learners focused on the content rather than the technology.

TYPES OF ONLINE COMMUNICATION

You will need to choose appropriate communication tools to enable an easy exchange between you and your learners and between learners. There are two basic modes of communication in the online environment: synchronous, which occurs at the same time, and asynchronous, which occurs at different times. Inter-actions can be one-to-one or one-to-many, depending on the type of tool. Both synchronous and asynchronous communications enable learners to collaborate with each other to exchange opinions, experiences, and interpretations of course content. The challenge is to provide the appropriate types of communication modes to help learners achieve the intended outcomes of a learning activity. Asynchronous communication enables learners and instructors to communicate anytime, anywhere, and thus offers flexibility to engage in the course materials at a time that fits with their lifestyle and commitments. The benefits of asynchronous communication include opportunities to think about course content and to address a diverse set of topics in more depth than can be done in a synchronous environment (Weasenforth, Biesenbach-Lucas, & Meloni, 2002). This creates an opportunity for learners to conceptualize a topic from multiple viewpoints and contribute to each other's understanding.

Jonathan Finkelstein (2006) describes five functions that real-time synchronous communication serves: instruction, collaboration, support, socialization, information exchanges, and extended outreach. Synchronous com-munication enables more dynamic communication because of the immediacy of the interaction. According to Finkelstein (2006), "the active construction of knowledge by learners through a process of real-time give-and-take is well-served in a live online setting" (p. 3). Synchronous communication provides a venue for instruction through real-time presentations and demonstrations. It enables learners to ask questions with an immediate response and follow-up questions to clarify understanding. Collaboration in the online environment through real-time synchronous communication gives immediacy of exchange and supports group work. Being able to provide just-in-time support through live interaction when learners have issues is critical to helping them persist. Opportunities for learners to socialize and develop interpersonal relationships can also increase motivation and help learners develop a network of peers to support one another. Finally, opportunities to extend reach beyond the classroom can increase motivation by providing learners with an opportunity to build a community.

There are some general characteristics of online interactions that need to be considered when choosing appropriates modes of communication. Interaction in an online environment is in some respects anonymous because it often hides the learner's identity. Many learners are attracted to the online environment because it puts them on the same level as other learners because their physical presence is unknown. Other learners are attracted to the online learning environment because they can add learning to their busy schedule by being able to participate anytime and anywhere. Synchronous communication modes may not meet the needs of learners who want to be anonymous or want to participate on their own schedule. In both synchronous and asynchronous communications, a learner's lack of good writing skills can also hinder his or her ability to communicate equally. In addition, if learners are not good typists, text communications in some synchronous environments may move too quickly for them to be able to keep up. As you begin to consider the types of interactions to support the learning outcomes of the course, it is important to understand that learners' ability to interact equally may be affected by their personal needs, time restrictions, and writing skills. Being able to offer learners a number of different types of communication modes can support the diversity of individual learning styles and help meet the needs of all learners.

There are a wide variety of communication tools for both asynchronous and synchronous communication. Choose an array of tools and technologies to develop presence, build community, and improve collaboration in your online course.

Chat or Instant Message

Chat or instant messaging is an excellent tool for generating communications on the fly. It requires a chat platform such as Google Chat, Yahoo! Messenger, and AOL Instant Messenger, and enables one-to-one and one-to-many communication (Manning & Johnson, 2011). Most course management systems have chat messenger technologies available. This form of communication is synchronous and, therefore, place and time dependent. It provides a spontaneous environment for learners to develop an "involvement" mode of presence through interactions with you and peers. It can be used in an online environment for virtual office hours and other personalized support for learners. In addition, it can be used as a tool for collaborating between learners and building community within a course. Some issues with chat relate to the speed at which messages appear and disappear, so it requires learners to have good typing skills as well as to be able to think quickly to continue engaging in the discussion. Learners who want more social presence in the course can use chat to talk informally with other learners when they are online at the same time. Thus it provides a social component of the learner-to-learner relationship, which can improve persistence by helping learners feel affiliation with their peers.

VoIP

VoIP stands for Voice over Internet Protocol whereby voice communications are delivered over an IP network such as the Internet. This technology allows synchronous one-to-one or one-to-many communications. Skype, Google Hangout, and Tinychat are a few examples of the VoIP tools available (Manning & Johnson, 2011). The technology has the capability of both voice and audio, so it can help develop greater presence with learners because they are able to see you during a conversation. It also has the capability of conferencing with a number of individuals in a single session for group interactions on projects and virtual office hours. VoIP is free, so learners can interact with you and peers without incurring costs. Currently, most computers come with built in audio and video; however, if learners are using an older computer they may have to purchase a webcam and speakers to use VoIP. One of the issues with VoIP can be the quality of the connection. Sometimes you may feel as though you are talking to someone in the next room; other times voices may fade in and out, thus diminishing communication and causing frustration.

Web Conferencing

Web conferencing is a synchronous one-to-one or one-to-many communication tool that enables a group to interact, share documents, make presentations, present demonstrations, and edit documents, to name a few of its applications. In addition, conferencing systems offer audio and video components to establish presence. Elluminate *Live!*, Adobe Connect, Dimdim, and Vyew are a few of the web conferencing tools available (Manning & Johnson, 2011). The value of a conferencing system is that it is live and provides opportunities for involvement and interaction by replicating the capabilities of the traditional face-to-face classroom. This is an excellent tool for you to use to deliver lectures with the opportunity for learners to interact during the presentation. It can also be used to demonstrate concepts that are more suitable for visual representation. Learners can also actively participate by asking questions. Web conferencing can be an excellent tool to use one-on-one with learners who are having difficulties because it enables the instructor to show the course environment and demonstrate to learners how to navigate the course. It can support group work by allowing teams to meet synchronously to go over a group project and discuss individual tasks and deliverables. It also supports construction of documents by enabling a team to have someone be the scribe while others edit as the group builds specific deliverables for the project. One of the obvious drawbacks is that it is time dependent, so everyone needs to be available to meet at the same time. This requirement can be challenging if learners are in different time zones and especially difficult if they are widely distributed throughout the world. In addition, there is a cost for a web conferencing as well as long distance fees for the telephone conference if your institution cannot provide a toll-free number. There are also limits to the number of learners who can actively interact in a live conference. If you use the built-in audio feature, everyone must have special equipment, such as a microphone. The video is great for establishing presence, but again, it requires everyone to have a camera for his or her computer.

E-mail

E-mail is an electronic mail tool that enables one-to-one or one-to-many communication. It is asynchronous, therefore not time and location dependent. More than likely you will have a course mail feature in your LMS; however, if a learner is not engaging in the course, you may also want to use e-mail to reach out to learners. There are free e-mail clients available including Pegasus and Eudora. E-mail can be used for learner-to-learner presence and faculty presence. You can provide personalized and continual feedback to learners with e-mail or a course mail feature. This enables learners to understand whether they are meeting the course expectations and provides an opportunity for interaction to help improve learners' performance. In addition, e-mail can be used among learners to involve them in collaborative projects to exchange ideas, share documents, and build relationships. Some e-mail clients, such as Microsoft Outlook, include tools that enable you to create distribution lists and template e-mail messages, so you can send communications to a number of individuals by using basic message templates, customized as needed. This can be a timesaver and ensures consistency in messaging.

As you develop your course in your LMS, be sure to connect with your institution, if you have not already, to determine the tools and support available to build your course. Also, search the Internet for tutorials and step-by-step instructions for building your course if you get stuck. Overall, as you build your course in the LMS, work through the elements thoroughly and patiently and don't be afraid to ask for help if you get stuck.

In this chapter, you reviewed key design principles to help you effectively organize your web environment or LMS. You also reviewed many options to integrate communication tools into your online course. Whether you are selecting your own tools or organizing your content in your institution's LMS, these principles and tools will help you ensure the technology you use to deliver your online course supports your learners and does not become a barrier to their persistence and success.

Action Steps

To help you apply the concepts in this chapter, complete the following:

- If you have not done so already, determine if your institution uses an LMS for online learning.
  - If so, determine what level of administrative rights you have. This will define to what extent you will be able to control the design of your course.
  - If not, review the purpose and outcomes of the course and the principles in the chapter to review and select an LMS or online tools to create your online course.
- Build the content of your course in your LMS and select online tools using the principles listed in the chapter. If you need assistance using your LMS or online tools, search for tutorials and job aids or contact your IT department to see if they provide assistance.

Implementation and Evaluation

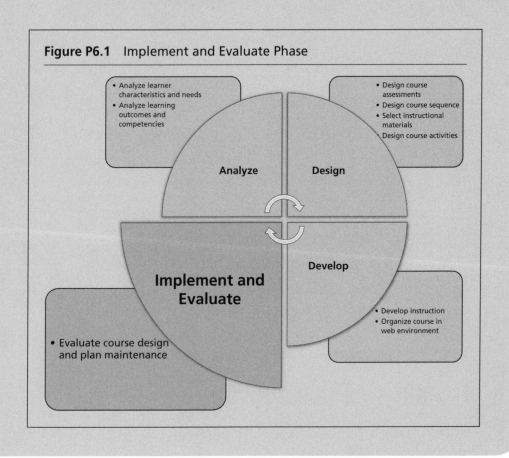

Figure P6.1 Implement and Evaluate Phase

- Analyze learner characteristics and needs
- Analyze learning outcomes and competencies

- Design course assessments
- Design course sequence
- Select instructional materials
- Design course activities

Analyze

Design

Implement and Evaluate

Develop

- Develop instruction
- Organize course in web environment

- Evaluate course design and plan maintenance

Part 6, "Implementation and Evaluation," introduces the last phases of the development process. Because the book is focused on course design, we will not discuss implementation strategies. However, we will discuss how to evaluate your course prior to implementation to ensure it meets quality standards for online courses. Chapter 12, "Course Evaluations and Maintenance," is the final chapter in the book and the only chapter in part 6. In this chapter, we help you conduct a final review of your course. We also discuss data collection post-implementation for the purpose of continuous quality improvement and finish up with a discussion of how to maintain your course over time.

Course Evaluations
and Maintenance

OBJECTIVES

After reviewing this chapter, you should be able to

- Review your course prior to implementation to ensure that all the components align to help learners successfully achieve the stated outcomes of the course.
- Create a plan to gather data for future course changes to improve learner persistence.
- Create a plan to maintain and continually improve your online course to support learner persistence.

Once you have completed the design of your online course, it is important to conduct a final review to ensure the course meets the expectations of your stated outcomes and is designed in a way to support learning. Once you have launched your course, you will also need to engage in continuous quality improvement and evaluate your learners' performance and achievement of competencies to ensure they are able to persist and achieve the course outcomes. This chapter focuses on strategies to help you evaluate your newly designed course and opportunities to engage in continuous quality improvement and perform maintenance strategies.

FINAL COURSE REVIEW

Before you launch your course, it is important to complete a final evaluation of the course to ensure it is aligned to the learning outcomes and has been designed effectively to achieve them. You will also want to make sure that you have used a variety of strategies to keep learners motivated and created clear instructions so learners can successfully complete the activities in the course and achieve the intended outcomes. Using elements of the Quality Matters (2011) rubric, the University of Chico Rubric for Online Instruction (ROI) (California State University, Chico, 2003), and our experience with online course design, we have developed an evaluation checklist in exhibit 12.1. The criteria are based on the principles we have described through the book, so it will be a good way to ensure you have effectively implemented the strategies discussed.

After spending so much time designing the course, you may experience tunnel vision and not be able to catch possible problems in the course; therefore, you may also want to ask a colleague to review your course using your checklist to provide you with additional suggestions for improving the course.

INSTRUCTIONAL SCAFFOLDING REVIEW

Throughout the design of your course, you have considered important strategies to support learner persistence. It is important to reflect on the activities you have designed in the course and ask yourself if you have successfully scaffolded them to ensure learners can meet expectations and successfully complete activities. Now that you have finished designing your course, consider the different types of scaffolding strategies in exhibit 12.2 to determine if you have included an appropriate level of scaffolding throughout to support learner success.

Using the evaluation tools we have presented will help you reflect on the design of your course and make appropriate adjustments to it before you interact with your learners.

CONTINUOUS QUALITY IMPROVEMENT

Learner performance data should be collected and used to understand the effectiveness of your course design across time in helping learners achieve the intended outcomes of the course. Assessment data can help you understand

Exhibit 12.1   Course Design Review Criteria

Criteria	Yes	No	Comments
Course Introduction			
Course follows university standards (insert specific standards in this review guide).			
On entering the course for the first time, learners can easily locate information to help them understand what to do (i.e., a "start here first" document).			
If your course is not based on a standard university template, you have provided a course orientation to the various course components and their function.			
There is an introduction to the course in the syllabus or faculty expectation statement describing the intended course outcomes.			
There is an introduction to how the course is structured in the syllabus or faculty expectation statement (e.g., how long units are, weekly activities, deadlines). This may also be included in a course orientation if you have developed one.			
There are clear expectations for learners in a syllabus or faculty expectation statement (including required days in the course per week, expectations for discussions, absences from course, policies including plagiarism, code of conduct, netiquette rules, due dates, and extensions).			
There is specific information about the minimum technical requirements for the course including hardware, software, and preferred browser. It also includes minimum technical skills needed to participate fully in the course (i.e., ability to create and save files, attach documents, etc.).			
The instructor clearly communicates expectations regarding how to communicate with him or her as well as turnaround time for returning learners' calls, and e-mails. There are also descriptions of expectations for when discussions and assignments will be graded and returned to learners.			
Course Outcomes, Competencies, and Objectives			
Course outcomes and competencies are clearly stated in a format that communicates the relevance of each outcome to the real world.			

(continued)

Exhibit 12.1 *(continued)*

Criteria	Yes	No	Comments
Learning objectives clearly align to course outcomes and competencies.			
Learning activities clearly align to course outcomes and objectives.			
Instructions to learners on how to meet the learning objectives are adequate and stated clearly.			
The prerequisite skills for the course are clearly stated and are reasonable and appropriate to the target population.			
Instructional Resources and Materials			
All instructional resources and materials map back to the stated program outcomes and competencies.			
Clear instructions help learners understand how the instructional resources support the achievement of specific competencies and objectives.			
The instructional materials are written at a level understandable to the learner population.			
All instructional resources and materials have all required copyright clearance.			
All instructional materials are accessible to all learners following ADA standards such as screen readability and alternative presentation of materials.			
Multimedia elements are relevant to the course competencies.			
Multimedia elements engage learners in the subject matter.			
The course effectively engages learners in the use of online resources.			
Instructional Strategies			
Instructional strategies promote critical thinking.			
Instructional strategies promote improvement of writing skills.			
Instructional strategies are relevant to real-world application.			
Clear instructions include an explanation of how course activities fit within the structure of the course and its intended outcomes.			

Exhibit 12.1 *(continued)*

Criteria	Yes	No	Comments
Assessment and Feedback			
Course assessments are relevant to real-world application.			
Assessments clearly align to course competencies.			
Scoring guide criteria clearly align to course competencies.			
Assessment strategies provide appropriate opportunity for learners to demonstrate content knowledge and skills.			
Assessment strategies provide appropriate opportunity for learners to demonstrate performance standards.			
Learners have opportunity for relevant practice prior to assessment of competencies.			
The course adequately prepares learners for practice activities.			
Learners have opportunity for formative evaluation prior to final assessment of competencies.			
The course adequately prepares learners for a final competency assessment.			
The course provides opportunities for instructor and peer feedback in a timely and consistent manner.			
Presence			
The course provides opportunities to develop social presence.			
The course provides opportunities to develop instructor presence.			
The course provides opportunities to develop cognitive presence.			
Course Structure			
The course structure is well organized with a clear and logical flow from one topic to the next.			
The course presentation is consistent throughout units. For each unit of study, there is consistency in the layout of course materials and activities, including consistency in the nomenclature for headings and other elements of the course.			

(continued)

Exhibit 12.1 (*continued*)

Criteria	Yes	No	Comments
Clear Instructions			
Instructions are clear and concise.			
Instruction is formatted for easy on-screen reading.			
Instruction includes templates, worksheets, and examples to support learner success.			
Course Workload			
The course contains an appropriate amount of coursework for the level of course (complete course workload map to determine this criterion).			
The course workload is consistent throughout the course (complete course workload map to determine this criterion).			
Use of Technology			
The course uses delivery methods appropriate to the learning activities.			
Learners have a clear understanding of the technology used in the course and how to use it.			
Learner Support and Resources			
The course provides links to appropriate academic support resources (e.g. library, writing center) to enhance the learning experience.			
The course includes information regarding learner support services to resolve administrative and technical issues.			
Overall Course Quality			
Use the following space to comment on the overall quality of the course and any items not covered in this checklist.			

Exhibit 12.2 Scaffolding Strategies to Support Learner Success

Scaffolding	Type	Description	Examples
Procedural	Orientation to course structure	Describe the organization of your online course environment including navigation elements, tools, and spaces.	Course orientation
	Start here first document	Document learner access during the first day of class to help learners determine steps for completing the activities.	Start here first
	Faculty expectations	Describes specific expectations for learners in your course, which helps them orient themselves to your teaching style, the weekly routine, policies, and engagement expectations.	Faculty expectations
	Course roadmap	Develop a one-page document that lays out the content of the course over the weeks and describes main topics, readings, discussions, and assignments.	Course roadmap
Metacognitive	Planning tools	What do I need to do?	• Course roadmap • Unit checklist
		How much time will I need?	• Unit checklist with time estimates • Unit checklist template
		What prior knowledge do I have?	• Advance organizer • Outline
	Monitoring tools	Rehearsal of learned information	• Discussions • Study questions • Flashcards • Puzzles
		Ensure learners are on the right track with major assignments.	Draft assignment
	Evaluation tools	Provide opportunities for learners to reflect on their performance.	• Peer review • Grading rubrics • Self-evaluation against grading criteria • Reflective questions
Conceptual	Worksheets	Provide opportunities to focus attention on important concepts.	• Vocabulary • Research analysis • Fill-in-the-blank study guides • Outline • Argument analysis • Problems • Scenarios

(continued)

Exhibit 12.2 (*continued*)

Scaffolding	Type	Description	Examples
	Templates	Provide clarity and focus for assignments.	• Paper template with focus on APA or other formatting styles • Paper template with focus on descriptive sections related to specific criteria learners will be graded on
	Knowledge maps	Provide opportunities for learners to create a visual picture to improve learning.	• Map showing relationship of important concepts • Fill-in-the-blank maps to help learners think through important relationships • Mapping tools to help learners organize information visually
Strategic	Instructor driven	Provide just-in-time support.	• Examples: worked, real world • Alternative explanations • Demonstration

particular activities in which learners do well and others in which they don't do as well. By reviewing performance data for trends and carefully reviewing associated course materials, instructions, formative assessments, and engagement, you may find important elements of the course you can change to improve performance. Instruction may need to be improved for clarity or you may need to add worksheets, templates, or examples to improve learner performance on graded activities.

You may also want to include instructional strategies that enable you to gather data from learners throughout the course such as muddiest point discussions, minute papers, or self-reflections that encourage learners to reflect on an activity and show areas in which they were confused, ineffective, or effective, as well as a number of other observations that you may not have expected. These comments can be used to understand specific issues that may be getting in the way of learner success and provide you with another layer of detail for revising and continually improving your course.

End-of-Course Evaluation Tool

Often, institutions have course evaluations that are based on learner satisfaction and learner perceptions of the course. Although learners typically have skewed perceptions of their own learning, time on task, and clarity of instructions, these types of questions can help you determine specific issues that learners experience during the course. Completing an evaluation at the midpoint of the course as well as the end will help you gather more information about your course and may help you capture just-in-time data to enable you to quickly make changes that may keep some learners from dropping out. If your institution does not have a standard learner course evaluation, exhibit 12.3 provides you an example of some questions to ask learners.

Other Data Points

You may also want to gather data on specific persistence variables. You can consider your course evaluation as an action research project. Review the audience analysis you completed in chapter 3 and determine which persistence variables are most applicable to your learners. To start, craft an evaluation based on the variables and then revise from there once you start receiving feedback. This will enable you to target the variables most likely to affect your learners and adjust as necessary. For instance, perhaps you find out that many learners work long hours during the week and based on course participation you see that they do the majority of their work on the weekend. Perhaps that information can be used to consider a course edit to help learners be more successful, for instance, by changing the assignment due dates. Also, connect with your institution's data analysis staff. They may gather data related to your course that could further support your evaluation efforts.

It may be helpful to run a single section of your course as a pilot and gather evaluation feedback to test the course with a smaller audience. This will help you get accustomed to facilitating your online course as well as provide an opportunity to gather more perspectives and information about your course before offering it to a broader audience.

SWOT Analysis

Once you have all of that information, it's time to analyze the inputs. If you have a research background, you may have a variety of data analysis strategies to choose

Exhibit 12.3   Learner End-of-Course Evaluation Template

Criteria	Rating (1–5) Agree to Strongly Agree	Comments
Course Organization		
The course content kept my attention throughout the quarter or semester.		
The course content was presented in an interesting style.		
The instructional text was easy to understand.		
The course was organized in a way that made it easy for me to engage in activities.		
Course Outcomes		
The course competencies and objectives were easy to understand.		
The course enabled me to build on my existing knowledge of the topic.		
The difficulty level of the course was appropriate to my knowledge level.		
The course enabled me to further develop my writing skills.		
The range of topics included in the course provided me a firm understanding of course concepts.		
The course materials were relevant to the course concepts.		
Course Pace and Workload		
The course workload was consistent throughout the course.		
The course workload was manageable throughout the course.		
The pace of the course was appropriate.		
Engagement		
Opportunities to interact with other learners were helpful to the learning process.		
Opportunities to interact with the instructor were helpful to the learning process.		

Exhibit 12.3   *(continued)*

Criteria	Rating (1–5) Agree to Strongly Agree	Comments
Assessments and Feedback		
The course assignments provided an opportunity to practice my understanding of the course concepts.		
The course assignments provided an opportunity to demonstrate my understanding of the course concepts.		
Feedback was provided throughout the course in a timely manner.		
The feedback provided was relevant and helpful to course concepts.		
Use of Technology		
Multimedia contributed to my understanding of course concepts.		
The course delivery methods were appropriate to course concepts.		
The course was easily accessible.		
The course delivery speed was adequate.		
Support Resources		
The course provided relevant links to additional resources (such as the library or writing center) to assist me in completing activities and assignments.		
The course included helpful information regarding learner support services available.		
Relevancy		
The course activities were relevant to real-world application.		
I will be able to apply the course concepts to my current workplace.		
Overall Course		
Use the following space to comment on your overall course experience and any additional ideas for improving the course.		

Exhibit 12.4   SWOT Analysis

	Strengths *What is working well?*	Weaknesses *What do learners seem to struggle with?*
Opportunities *Where could we make additional improvements?*	Opportunity—strength strategies (Use strengths to take advantage of opportunities)	Opportunity—weakness strategies (Overcome weaknesses by taking advantage of opportunities)
Threats *Have you noticed learner drop out? Why do they drop out?*	Threat—strength strategies (Use strengths to avoid threats)	Threat—weakness strategies (Minimize weaknesses and avoid threats)

Source: Adapted from David (1993).

from once you have your data collected. A strengths, weaknesses, opportunities, and threats (SWOT) analysis provides an easy way to analyze your data using a format that helps facilitate course improvements. Exhibit 12.4 shows a way to look at the analysis from a matrix perspective.

In the strengths box, list what is working well in your course such as which outcomes learners are performing really well on, engaging course activities, or resources learners comment are especially helpful. In the weaknesses box, list what is not working well in your course that learners are struggling with such as assignments learners have a lot of questions about, outcomes learners are performing poorly on, or difficult instructional materials or activities. In the opportunities box, list areas in which you could make additional improvements such as clarifying assignments or activity instructions, swapping out instructional materials, or providing additional scaffolding. In the threats box, list the reasons that learners drop out such as financial aid issues, difficulty of activities, or lack of relevance.

Once you complete those outer boxes, you move to the middle boxes. In the opportunity—strength strategies box, identify strategies to leverage the strengths of your course to take advantage of opportunities. For instance, if you see that an assignment template is working really well for one assessment, you could use that successful one for additional assignments. In the opportunity—weakness strategies box, identify strategies for which you can overcome your weaknesses by making an improvement. For example, you could identify activities learners understand well and revise activities in which learners are struggling to align with those characteristics. In the threat—strength strategies box, identify how you may use your strengths to avoid your threats. For instance, if you communicate the relevance of the course to learners' fields of study well in the course introduction, perhaps you can integrate similar relevancy information in each of the course activities that learners are finding are not as relevant to their personal and professional goals. Finally, in the threat—weakness strategies box, identify strategies that will help you minimize weaknesses and avoid threats. For example, if learners are having financial aid problems and cannot purchase materials prior to the course start, use library and web resources in the first couple of units.

Once you have your analysis complete, prioritize the opportunities for revision and complete a few changes so you can determine if the changes actually helped learners improve. If you make too many revisions to your course at once, you may be unable to determine if what you changed actually improved persistence or if you changed elements that actually hurt persistence. First, implement any changes that seem like easy wins or low-hanging fruit. Select those revisions that are the most frequently mentioned and are the most straightforward. Examples may include the need for more specific instruction for assignments and activities in which learners have a lot of questions, or, perhaps, adding more scaffolding for specific readings that learners struggled with, such as a study guide or study questions to answer as learners complete the readings. Prioritize revisions that you feel will have the biggest impact on your learners' persistence. Some items that may jump out at you are objectives or outcomes in which many learners are not performing well, certain activities that learners are not completing, or a unit of the course in which you saw the most drops. Resist the urge to completely restructure or redesign your whole course. Small, successive changes will help you get closer to understanding your learners' persistence variables and how your specific revisions are improving their success.

COURSE MAINTENANCE

Another element to consider in addition to continual improvement is course maintenance. As you review your course for improvements, you will also want to review the course to ensure your content is up-to-date and still accessible. Web resources are continually in flux and web pages, articles, and multimedia, may be moved at any time. As we mentioned in the chapter 8 discussion of course materials, it is good to evaluate the stability of resources before you decide to use them in the course. You also want to check your links each quarter to make sure your resources are still accessible. Review your course materials to see if there are any newer resources that better represent the information. If you are in a field that is constantly changing, you are probably already aware of the importance of keeping up-to-date on new research findings and integrating them into your course.

In this chapter, we discussed strategies to evaluate, maintain, and continually improve your online course to support learner persistence. These strategies will become essential to refining your course to meet the needs of your learners. Each time you facilitate your online course, you will likely learn new characteristics of your learners, different strategies to help them persist, and the effectiveness of your course design and content. To continue to support your learners' persistence, it is important to review these lessons and incorporate them into the design of your course.

Action Steps

To help you apply the concepts in this chapter, complete the following:

- Use exhibit 12.1 to review your course and make any adjustments, as necessary, prior to initial implementation of the course.
- Use exhibit 12.2 to review the instructional scaffolding in your course and make any adjustments to further support learners' achievement of course learning outcomes.
- Make a plan to collect and use learner performance data to evaluate and continually improve your online course.
- Create a learner evaluation or revise exhibit 12.3 to gather data from your learners about the course to help improve the course for future iterations.
- Create a plan to use exhibit 12.4 or a method of your choice to analyze and prioritize your data and potential revisions.
- Create a plan for course maintenance.

Final Remarks

Well we've come to the end of our journey. We hope that the information we have provided in this book has given you a strong foundation and solid process and structure to design your online course. If you have not accessed *A Guide to Online Course Design: Strategies for Student Success*, which accompanies the text, please go to www.josseybass.com/go/stavredes_herder. This guide includes all of the steps we have discussed in the book to create your online course along with worksheets to help you think through each of the steps of the process.

As you move forward to implementing and teaching your online course, we recommend that you look at *Effective Online Teaching: Foundations and Strategies for Student Success* (Stavredes, 2011) for additional pedagogical strategies to implement in your teaching. It also contains additional resources that may be valuable as you design your course. We hope this book has helped you successfully design your online course, and we wish you the best at implementation!

References

Allen, I. E., & Seaman, J. (2010). *Class differences: Online education in the United States, 2010.* Babson Survey Research Group. Retrieved from http://sloanconsortium.org/publications/survey/pdf/class_differences.pdf

Allen, I. E., & Seaman, J. (2013). *Changing course: Ten years of tracking online education in the United States.* San Francisco: Babson Survey Research Group and Quahog Research Group.

American Association of Law Libraries. (2005). *Writing learning outcomes.* Retrieved from www.aallnet.org/prodev/outcomes.asp

American Psychological Association. (2010). *Publication manual of the American Psychological Association* (6th ed.). Washington, DC: Author.

Anderson, L. W., & Krathwohl, D. R. (Eds.). (2001). *A taxonomy for learning, teaching and assessing: A revision of Bloom's taxonomy of educational objectives* (Complete ed.). New York: Longman.

Ausubel, D. P. (1960). The use of advance organizers in the learning and retention of meaningful verbal material. *Journal of Educational Psychology, 51,* 267–272.

Ausubel, D. (1963). *The psychology of meaningful verbal learning.* New York: Grune & Stratton.

Barker, A. M. (2002). A case study in instructional design for web-based courses. *Nursing Education Perspectives, 23*(4), 183–186.

Barrows, H. S., & Kelson, A. M. (1993). *Problem-based learning: A total approach to education.* Springfield: Southern Illinois University School of Medicine.

Bean, J. R., & Metzner, B. (1985). A conceptual model of nontraditional undergraduate student attrition. *Review of Educational Research, 55,* 485–650.

Billings, D. M. (1988). A conceptual model of correspondence course completion. *American Journal of Distance Education, 2*(2), 23–35.

Blair-Early, A., & Zender, M. (2008). User interface design principles for interaction design. *Design Issues, 24*(3).

Bloom, B., Englehart, M., Furst, E., Hill, W., & Krathwohl, D. (1956). *Taxonomy of educational objectives: The classification of educational goals. Handbook I: Cognitive domain.* New York: Longmans, Green.

Bransford, J. D., Brown, A. L., & Cocking, R. R. (Eds.). (2000). *How people learn: Brain, mind, experience, and school* (Expanded ed.). Washington, DC: The National Academies Press.

Brogden, L., & Couros, A. (2002). Contemplating the virtual campus: Pedagogical and administrative considerations. *The Delta Kappa Gamma Bulletin, 68*(3), 22–30.

Brookfield, S. D. (1987). *Developing critical thinkers. Challenging adults to explore alternative ways of thinking and acting.* San Francisco: Jossey-Bass.

Brookfield, S. D., & Preskill, S. N. (2005). *Discussion as a way of teaching: Tools and techniques for democratic classrooms.* San Francisco: Jossey-Bass.

California State University, Chico. (2003). *Rubric for online instruction.* Retrieved from www.csuchico.edu/celt/roi/index.shtml

Cohen, A. S., & Wollack, J. A. (n.d.). *Handbook on test development: Helpful tips for creating reliable and valid classroom tests.* Testing & Evaluation Services, University of Wisconsin-Madison. Retrieved from http://testing.wisc.edu/Handbook%20on%20Test%20Construction.pdf

Council for Higher Education Accreditation. (2001). *Accreditation and student learning outcomes: A proposed point of departure.* Retrieved from www.chea.org/award/StudentLearningOutcomes2001.pdf

Cyrs, T. E. (1997). Competence in teaching at a distance. In R. E. Weiss, J. Knowlton, & B. W. Speck (Eds.), *Principles of effective teaching in the online classroom* (pp. 15–18). San Francisco: Jossey-Bass.

Dabbagh, N. (2003). Scaffolding: An important teacher competency in online teaching. *TechTrends, 47*(2), 39–44.

David, F. R. (1993). *Strategic management* (4th ed.). New York: Macmillan.

Digital Millennium Copyright Act, P.L. 105–304, 112 Stat. 2860 (1998).

Dray, B. J., Lowenthal, P. R., Miszkiewics, M. J., Ruiz-Primo, M. A., & Marczynski, K. (2011). Developing an instrument to assess student readiness for online learning: A validation study. *Distance Education, 32*(1), 29–47.

Elder, L., & Paul, R. (2010). *The thinker's guide to analytic thinking.* Dillon Beach, CA: Foundation for Critical Thinking Press.

Finkelstein, J. (2006). *Learning in real time. Synchronous teaching and learning online.* San Francisco: Jossey-Bass.

Garrison, D. R., Anderson, T., & Archer, W. (2000). Critical inquiry in a text-based environment: Computer conferencing in higher education. *The Internet and Higher Education, 2*(2–3), 87–105.

Green, K. C. (2010, November). *Managing online education*. Encino, CA: The Campus Computing Project/WCET.

Grosse, C. U. (2004). How distance learning changes faculty. *International Journal of Instructional Technology and Distance Learning, 1*(6). Retrieved from www.itdl.org /journal/jun_04/june_04.pdf

Hacker, D., & Sommers, N. (2011). *A writer's reference with strategies for online learners* (7th ed.). New York: Macmillan.

Hanna, W. (2007). The new Bloom's taxonomy: Implications for music education. *Arts Education Policy Review, 108*(4), 7–16.

Hannifin, M., Land, S., & Oliver, K. (1999). Open learning environments: Foundations, methods and models. In C. M. Reigeluth (Ed.), *Instructional-design theories and models: A new paradigm of instructional theory* (pp. 115–140). Mahwah, NJ: Lawrence Erlbaum.

Horton, W. (2012). *E-learning by design* (2nd ed.). San Francisco: Pfeiffer.

Illinois Online Network. (1998–2006). *Quality online course initiative*. Retrieved from www.ion.uillinois.edu/initiatives/qoci/rubric.asp

Kember, D. (1995). *Open learning for adults: A model of student progress*. Englewood Cliffs, NJ: Educational Technology Publications.

Kolb, D. A. (1976). *The learning style inventory: Technical manual*. Boston: McBer.

Kolb, D. A. (1999). *Learning style inventory, Version 3*. Boston: Hay Group.

Kozlowski, D. (2004). Factors for consideration in the development and implementation of an online RN-BSN course: Faculty and student perceptions. *CIN: Computers, Informatics, Nursing, 22*(1), 34–43.

Krug, S. (2006). *Don't make me think: A common sense approach to web usability* (2nd ed.). Indianapolis: New Riders.

Lehman, R. M., & Conceicão, S.C.O. (2010). *Creating a sense of presence in online teaching. How to "be there" for distance learners*. San Francisco: Jossey-Bass.

Levine, A., & Sun, J. (2002). *Barriers to distance education*. Washington, DC: American Council on Education Center for Policy Analysis.

Link, D., & Scholtz, S. (2000). Educational technology and faculty role: What you don't know can hurt you. *Nurse Educator, 25*(6), 274–276.

Lorenzetti, J. P. (2004). Changing faculty perceptions of online workload. *Distance Education Report, 8*(20), 1–6.

Manning, S., & Johnson, K. (2011). *The technology toolbelt for teaching*. San Francisco: Jossey-Bass.

Mayer, R. E. (2001). *Multimedia learning*. New York: Cambridge University Press.

Mayer, R. E., & Moreno, R. (n.d.). *A cognitive theory of multimedia learning: Implications for design principles*. Retrieved from http://spnd423.com/SPND%20423%20Readings /A%20Cognitive%20Theory.pdf

Miller, G. A. (1956). The magical number seven, plus or minus two: Some limits on our capacity for processing information. *Psychological Review, 63*(2), 81–97.

Mills, M. E., Fisher, C., & Stair, N. (2001). Web-based courses. *Nursing and Health Care Perspective, 22*(5), 235–239.

Monterey Institute for Technology and Education. (2010). Online course evaluation project. Retrieved from www.montereyinstitute.org/pdf/OCEP%20Evaluation%20Categories.pdf

Morrison, G. R., Ross, S. M., Kalman, H. K., & Kemp, J. E. (2011). *Designing effective instruction* (6th ed.). Hoboken, NJ: Wiley.

Noel-Levitz. (2012). *National online learners priorities report.* Retrieved from www.noellevitz.com/papers-research-higher-education/2011/2011-adult-and-online-learner-satisfaction-priorities-reports

Oblinger, D., & Hawkins, B. (2006). The myth about online course development. *Educause Review, 41*(1), 14–15.

O'Neill, M. S. (1998). Developing and implementing an online nursing course. *Online Journal of Distance Learning Administration, 1*(4). Retrieved from www.westga.edu/~distance/ojdla/winter14/oneill14.html

Palloff, R. M., & Pratt, K. (2003). *The virtual student: A profile and guide to working with online learners.* San Francisco: Jossey-Bass.

Palloff, R. M., & Pratt, K. (2009). *Assessing the online learner: Resources and strategies for faculty.* San Francisco: Jossey-Bass.

Pankowski, M. (2008). Training and support for online faculty in postsecondary institutions. In K. McFerrin et al. (Eds.), *Proceedings of Society for Information Technology and Teacher Education International Conference 2008* (pp. 633–636). Chesapeake, VA: AACE.

Paul, R., & Elder, L. (2009). *Miniature guide to critical thinking: Concepts and tools.* Dillon Beach, CA: Foundation for Critical Thinking.

Picciano, A. G. (2002). Beyond student perceptions: Issues of interaction, presence and performance in an online course. *Journal of Asynchronous Learning Networks, 6*(1), 21–40.

Picciano, A. G., Seaman, J., & Allen, I. (2010). Educational transformation through online learning: To be or not to be. *Journal of Asynchronous Learning Networks, 14*(4), 17–35.

Quality Matters. (2011). *About us.* Retrieved from www.qmprogram.org/about

Quality Matters. (2011–2013). *Higher ed program >Rubric.* Retrieved from www.qmprogram.org/rubric

Rockwell, K., Schauer, J., Fritz, S. M., & Marx, D. B. (1999). Incentives and obstacles influencing higher education faculty and administrators to teach via distance. *Online Journal of Distance Learning Administration, 2*(4), 98.

Rovai, A. P. (2003). In search of higher persistence rates in distance education online programs. *The Internet and Higher Education, 6*(1), 1–16.

Ryan, M., Carlton, K. H., & Ali, N. S. (2004). Reflections on the role of faculty in distance learning and changing pedagogies. *Nursing Education Perspectives, 25*(2), 73–80.

Savery, J. R., & Duffy, T. M. (1995). Problem-based learning: An instructional model and its constructivist framework. In B. Wilson (Ed.), *Constructivist learning environments: Case studies in instructional design* (pp. 135–148). Englewood Cliffs, NJ: Educational Technology Publications.

Schrum, L. (2002). On-line education: A study of emerging pedagogy. *New Directions for Adult and Continuing Education, 78*, 53–61.

Schunk, D. H., & Zimmerman, B. J. (1994). *Self-regulation of learning and performance: Issues and educational applications.* Hillsdale, NJ: Lawrence Erlbaum.

Sloan Consortium. (2013, January). *Changing course: Ten years of tracking online education in the United States.* Retrieved from http://sloanconsortium.org/publications /survey/changing_course_2012

Stavredes, T. M. (2011). *Effective online teaching: Foundations and strategies for student success.* San Francisco: Jossey-Bass.

Suskie, L. (2009). *Assessing student learning: A common sense guide* (2nd ed.). San Francisco: Jossey-Bass.

Technology, Education, and Copyright Harmonization Act, P.L. 107–273, 13301 (2002).

Tennant, M. (1997). *Psychology of adult learning.* London: Routledge.

Tinto, V. (1975). Dropout from higher education: A theoretical synthesis of recent research. *Review of Educational Research, 45*, 89–125.

United Nations Education, Scientific, and Cultural Organization. (2012). *Open educational resources.* Retrieved from www.unesco.org/new/en/communication-and -information/access-to-knowledge/open-educational-resources

US Congress (1998a, August 7). Section 504 of the Rehabilitation Act (29 U.S.C. 794), as amended by the Workforce Investment Act of 1998 (P.L. 105–220).

US Congress (1998b, August 7). Section 508 of the Rehabilitation Act (29 U.S.C. 794d), as amended by the Workforce Investment Act of 1998 (P.L. 105–220).

US Copyright Office. (2007). *Law and policy.* Retrieved from www.copyright.gov/laws

US Department of Education. (2006). *A test of leadership: Charting the future of U.S. higher education: A report of the commission appointed by Secretary of Education Margaret Spellings.* Retrieved from www2.ed.gov/about/bdscomm/list /hiedfuture/reports/final-report.pdf

Vygotsky, L. S. (1978). *Mind in society.* Cambridge, MA: Harvard University Press.

Weasenforth, D., Biesenbach-Lucas, S., & Meloni, C. (2002). Realizing constructivist objectives through collaborative technologies: Threaded discussions. *Language Learning & Technology, 6*(3), 58–86. Retrieved from http://llt.msu.edu/vol6num3 /pdf/vol6num3.pdf

West, J. A., & West, M. L. (2009). *Using wikis for online collaboration: The power of the read-write web.* Hoboken, NJ: Wiley.

Wiggins, G., & McTighe, J. (2005). *Understanding by design* (expanded 2nd ed.). Alexandria, VA: Association for Supervision and Curriculum Development.

Workman, J. J., & Stenard, R. A. (1996). Student support services for distance learners. *DEOSNEWS, 6*(3). Retrieved from www.ed.psu.edu/acsde/deos/deosnews/deosnews6_3.asp

Index

of, 73–75; strategies for, 63; summative *versus* formative, 54–55; types of, 55–61; use of, for continuous quality improvement, 174, 180. *See also* Formative assessments; Summative assessments

Assignments: instructions for, 147–149; of readings and presentations, 145–146; scaffolding, 149; scoring guides for, 149–153; unit, 147–153. *See also* Instructional activities

Assimilators, 84, 85

Assumptions, 128

Asynchronous communication: pros and cons of, 165–167; tools for, 169

Attitudes: assessment of, 57; definition and aspects of, 38, 40; types of, 37

Attrition rates, 4, 26. *See also* Dropping out; Persistence

Audacity, 103, 104

Audience analysis: conducting, 23, 24–29; needs analysis and, 29–30; outcome statements and, 46; sequence of instruction and, 70

Audio recording, 103, 104

Auditory channel, of brain, 98, 101

Ausubel, D. P., 89

Authentic, performance-based assessments, 55–56, 64–65

Automaticity, 119

Avatars, 123

Avons, 121

B

Backward design framework, 14–15. *See also* Design

Barker, A. M., xvii

Barrows, H. S., 132–133

Bean, J. R., 6–7, 24–25, 28, 81

Biesenbach-Lucas, S., 166

Billings, D. M., 5

Billings persistence model, 5

Blackboard, 124

Blair-Early, A., 162–164, 165

Blended instruction, 4

Blogger, 124

Blogs, 124

Bloom, B., 38, 116

Bloom's taxonomy: activities design and, 116, 119, 120, 130, 135; elements of, 37–40; verbs of, 40, 41

Brain processing, multimedia principles and, 98–101

Bransford, J. D., 80, 88

Breadcrumbs, 163

Breadth questions, 129

Brogden, L., xvii–xviii

Brookfield, S. D., 57, 123, 124

Brown, A. L., 80, 88

Business proposal, 63

C

California State University, Chico, 9, 174

Camtasia, 104, 105

Capstone course, 57

Carlton, K. H., xviii

Carnegie unit, 140

Case study activities, 63, 126

Changing Course (Allen & Seaman), xvii

Chat, online, 167–168

Chunking, 100

Clarity questions, 129

CmapTools, 104, 106

Cocking, R. R., 80, 88

Cognitive domain (knowledge), 38, 39

Cognitive learning styles, 83–86. *See also* Learning style preferences

Cognitive map, 164

Cognitive overload, 89

Cognitive presence, 82, 129, 177

Cognitive scaffolding strategies. *See* Scaffolding strategies

Cohen, A. S., 61

Coherence, 101

Collaborative assessments, 56, 57–58

Collaborative learning, 81; online communication tools for, 165–170; and problem solving, 126. *See also* Discussion

Collaborative workspaces, 134–135

Communication, online: principles of, 165–167; synchronous *versus* asynchronous, 165–167; tools for, 167–170

Community of inquiry model, 82–83, 125, 128–129

Competencies: activity alignment with, 116, 117–118; brainstorming, 40–43, 44; connecting to, in unit introduction, 145; course analysis for, 40–43, 44; learner evaluation of, 182; practice activities for, 118–123; review criteria for, 175–176; sequence of instruction and, 70–71; statements of, 37, 46–47; taxonomies of learning and, 37–40. *See also* Learning outcomes; Skills

Comprehension activities, 120–121

Computer-based interaction skills, minimum requirements for, 26, 27

Conceição, S.C.O., 121

Concept mapping: as content design element, 165; for course development, 42–43, 44; for learners, 85, 97–98, 106

Concepts, as thought elements, 128

Duffy, T. M., 132
Dzuiban, 24

E

E-mail, 169
Easy wins, 185
Economic downturn, xvii
Economics Network, 122
Edublogs, 124
Effective Online Teaching: Foundations and Strategies for Student Success (Stavredes), 112, 133, 187
Elder, L., 93, 125–129, 147
Electronic forms, 113
Electronic mail, 169
Elements of thought, 125–128
Elluminate *Live!*, 168
Employment responsibilities, 24, 28, 31, 181
End-of-course evaluation tool, 181, 182–183
Engagement: community of inquiry model to support, 82–83; content design to support, 165; discussion activities and, 124–130, 131; importance of, 81–82; interface design to support, 165; learner evaluation of, 182. *See also* Collaborative learning; Discussion; Interaction
Englehart, M., 38
English writing course example: assessment strategies for, 59–61, 64–66; competency statements for, 47; curriculum analysis for, 36; free writing for, 42; instructional materials for, 92–93; instructional strategies mapping worksheet for, 117–118; outcome statements for, 45–46; scoring guides for, 151, 152; sequencing for, 70–71, 72–73; test blueprint for, 59–61
Environment, course. *See* Online course environment
Environmental/external factors, in persistence, 28–29
Ethnicity, 25, 30
Eudora, 169
Evaluate phase, 18, 171–172, 173–185
Evaluation: as action research project, 181; action steps on, 186; assessment data used for, 174, 180; checklist and criteria for, 174, 175–178; continuous quality improvement, 174, 180–185; course maintenance and, 185–186; end-of-course survey, 181, 182–183; final course review, 174, 175–178; of instructional materials, 106–107, 108, 112, 176; instructional scaffolding review, 174, 179–180; overview of, 18, 171–172; with persistence variables, 181; phase of, 18, 171–172, 173–185; pilot course for, 181; revision strategies and, 185; SWOT analysis for, 181, 184–185; tools for scaffolding, 179
Evaluative questions, 125
Expectations, clarity of, 153, 154, 179
Experimentation strategies, 84, 85

F

Face-to-face instruction: defined, 3–4; online instruction *versus*, 26, 58–59, xix; testing in, 58–59
Faculty development: need for, xvii–xix; quality initiatives and, 8–9. *See also* Instructors
Faculty expectations statement, 154, 179
Fair Use Act, 107, 109, 111
Fairness questions, 129
Family responsibilities, 24, 31
Fantage, 123
Feedback: checklist and criteria for, 177; e-mail for, 169; formative assessments for, 54–55, 119; learner evaluation of, 183. *See also* Formative assessments
Field trips, virtual, 97
Final capstone course, 57
Final course review, 174, 175–178
Final Cut Pro, 104, 105
Final exam, 55
Finances, learner: instructional materials selection and, 94; as learner characteristic, 28, 30; web conferencing costs and, 169
Finkelstein, J., 166
Fisher, C., xvii
Flashcard Machine, 120
Flashcards, 120
Flexibility, 24
Flickr, 104, 106
Fonts, 158
Formative assessments: characteristics of, 54–55; comprehension activities for, 120; English writing course examples of, 66; practice activities for, 119; selection of, 61–65; sequencing of, 73–75; strategies and types of, 63
Free writing, 41–42
Freeman, 121
Fritz, S. M., xviii
Functional requirements of web-based information, 112, 113
Furst, E., 38

G

Garrison, D. R., 82–83, 125, 155
Gender, 25, 30

Goal commitment, 155

Go!Animate, 104, 106

Google Chat, 167

Google Cultural Institute, 97

Google Docs, 134

Google Hangout, 168

GPA, prior, 25, 30

Grading guides. *See* Scoring guides

Grading rubric, for critical thinking, 130, 131, 146–147

Green, K. C., xvii

Grosse, C. U., xviii

Grow, 7

Guide to Online Course Design, A: Strategies for Student Success (Stavredes and Herder), 18–19, 187

H

Hacker, D., 92

Handbook on Test Development (Cohen and Wollack), 61

Hands-on experience, 122

Hannifin, M., 87, 88, 149

Hawkins, B., xviii

Headings, 157, 163, 165

Herder, T., 187

High schools, virtual, xx

Higher education institutions: pressures and demands on, 3, 33–34, xvii, xviii–xix; reform of, 33–34

Higher-order skills: activities for, 116, 119, 121–123, 121–135; assessment of, 56. *See also* Critical thinking skills; Problem-solving skills

Hill, W., 38

Hints, 89

Horton, W., 93, 119, 122

How People Learn (Bransford, Brown, Cocking), 80

HTML 5 technology, 104, 106

I

Ijsselsteinjn, 121

Illinois Online Network, 8–9

Image creation and collection, 104, 106

Immersion, in virtual environment, 121, 122, 123

IMovie, 104, 106

Implement phase, 17–18, 171–172

Implementation: final course review prior to, 174, 175–178; overview of, 17–18, 171–172; phase of, 17–18, 171–172

Implications, 128

"In the news" discussion activity, 126

Inference, 127

Information, as thought element, 127

Information literacy skills, 26, 27, 134

Information-processing system (brain), 98–101

Initiative, 133

Inquiry: community of, 82–83, 125, 128–129; WebQuest strategy for, 133–134. *See also* Questions

Inspiration (image creation application), 104, 106

Instant messaging, 167–168

Institutional resources: checklist and criteria for, 178; for course evaluation, 181; multimedia, 102, 103; for online course development, 170; orienting learners to, 154, 156; text-based, 94

Instruction, development of. *See* Development, instructional

Instructional activities: action steps on, 136; alignment of, 116–118; comprehension, 120–121; connecting with, in unit introduction, 145; design of, 115–136; discussion, 124–130, 131; hands-on, 122; high-level, 116, 119, 121–135; mapping worksheet for, 116–118, 136; persistence and, 84, 85–86; practice, 118–123; problem-based, 130–132; real-world, 116, 119, 121–123, 130, 132–133; reflective, 123–124; role of, 115–116; unit organization for, 145–147; virtual practice, 121–123; WebQuest, 133–134

Instructional design process (ADDIE): action steps on, 20; analyze phase of, 16, 21–50; backward design framework and, 14–15, 16; cycle of, 18–19; design phase of, 16–19, 51–136; develop phase of, 17, 137–170; evaluate phase of, 18, 173–185; figure of, 18, 19; implement phase of, 17–18, 173–174; iterative, 78; online guide for, 18–19, 187; overview of, 13–20; phases of, 16–19; resources on, 18–19, 187; to support persistence, 16. *See also* Course development

Instructional materials: accessibility of, 110, 112; action steps on, 114; checklist for, 107, 108, 176; connection with, in unit introduction, 145; copyright clearance for, 107, 109–110, 111; criteria for, 106–107, 108, 176; in English course example, 92–93; evaluation of, 106–107, 108, 112, 176; maintenance of, 185–186; multimedia, 96–106, 108; open educational, 95–96; purpose of, 91, 93; quality standards for, 10; review criteria for, 176; selection of, 91–114; text-based, 94–95, 108. *See also* Multimedia

Instructional strategies: action steps on, 90, 114, 136; checklist and criteria for, 176; cognitive scaffolding strategies and, 86–90; design of, 77–136; engagement principles and, 81–83; instructional activities and, 115–136; instructional materials and, 91–114; learning style preferences and, 83–86; mapping worksheet, 116–118, 136; principles of learning and, 80–81; quality standards for, 10; theoretical foundations for, 79–90

Instructions: assignment, 147–149; checklist and criteria for, 176, 178; guidelines for writing, 156–158; quality standards for clear, 11

Instructors: need for professional development of, 8–9, xvii–xix; responsibility of, for online course development, xvii–xix; teaching presence of, 83, 167, 168, 177

Integrity, in team, 58

Intellectual standards, 128–129

Interaction: community of inquiry model for, 82–83; discussion activities and, 124–130, 131; learning style preferences and, 85; online communication tools for, 165–170; personal introductions for, 155; skill requirements for, 26, 27. *See also* Collaborative learning; Discussion; Engagement

Interface: clear reverse in, 163; consistent logic in, 163, 165; cultural differences and, 164; defined, 162; design principles for, 162–164; importance of, 161–162; landmarks in, 164; obvious start in, 162–163; proximity of elements in, 164; standard practice conventions in, 164; to support engagement, 165

Interpretation, 127

Introduction: course, 10, 11, 153–156, 175; to course outcomes, 154–155; personal, 155; to processes and guides, 156; unit, 144–145

Involvement, in virtual environment, 121

ITunes U, 102, 105

J

Jing, 104, 105

Johnson, K., 123, 124, 134, 167, 168

Josseybass.com/go/stavredes_herder, 187

Just-in-time strategies, 54, 87, 166, 180, 181

K

Kelson, A. M., 132–133

Kember, D., 5–6

Kember persistence model, 5–6

Kerka, 7

Khan Academy, 102

Knowledge: comprehension activities for, 120–121; definition and aspects of, 37–38, 39; problem-based learning for, 133; types of, 37

Knowledge maps, 97–98, 180

Kolb, D. A., 83

Kolb Learning Style Inventory (LSI), 83–85

Kozlowski, D., xvii

Krathwohl, D. R., 38

Krug, S., 165

L

Land, S., 87, 88, 149

Landmarks, 164

Language: conciseness of, 165; for describing learning outcomes, 43, 45, 49; for instructions, 157

Learn Out Loud, 102

Learner attrition model, 6

Learner characteristics: analysis of, 23, 24–29; environmental factors and, 28–29; key questions for identifying, 25; needs analysis based on, 29–31; outcome statements and, 46; persistence and, 6, 7, 24–29; skill requirements and, 25–28; in United States, 24

Learner developmental pathways, 69–71

Learner-institution fit, 6

Learner needs: analysis of, 23, 29–31; learner characteristics and, 29–31; listed, 30–31; persistence and, 7–8, 29

Learner persistence. *See* Persistence

Learner readiness, 26, 28

Learner satisfaction and perceptions: end-of-course evaluation survey of, 181, 182–183; measure, 8

Learner skill requirements: listed, 27; minimum, 25–28

Learners goals: connecting course with, 154–155; key needs based on, 30

Learning: active, 80–81, 132; preexisting knowledge and, 80; principles of, 80–81; with understanding, 80

Learning management systems (LMSs): administrative rights to, 162, 170; blog tools in, 124; consistent logic in, 163, 165; e-mail feature in, 169; minimizing distractions in, 165; navigation bar options in, 162–163; quiz features in, 120. *See also* Online course environment

Learning outcomes: action steps on, 50; alignment of, to program of study, 35–37; analysis of, 33–50; assessments alignment with, 59–61, 62, 64–66, 150; assessments design for, 53–67; brainstorming, 40–43, 44; breaking down, into competencies, 46–47; competencies and, 37–43, 46–47; components of, 45; connecting to, in course introduction, 154–155; course analysis for, 40–43, 44; criteria for, 48–49, 175–176; curriculum analysis and, 35–37, 43; defined, 34; development of, 33–50; in English course example, 45–46; final course review for alignment with, 174, 175–178; importance of, 33–34; instructional activities alignment with, 116, 117–118; language for describing, 43, 45, 49; learner evaluation of, 182; number of, 46; quality standards for, 10; sequence of instruction and, 70–71; statements of, 43, 45–46, 48–49, 144; taxonomies of learning and, 37–40. *See also* Outcome statements; Outcomes-based curriculum

Learning style preferences: classification of, 83–85; instructional activities to support, 84, 85–86; instructional materials to support, 93, 98; multimedia and, 98, 99; strategic scaffolding and, 89

Learning taxonomies, 37–40

Lectures, 96, 98, 168

Lehman, R. M., 121

Letter writing, 126

Levine, A., xviii

Library, online, 26

Life crises, 28, 31

Link, D., xviii

Links, 163, 186

Lists, bulleted and numbered, 157

Literacy skills, 26, 27

Literary analysis paper, 63

Logic questions, 129

Long-term memory, 99, 100

Lorenzetti, J. P., xviii

Lowenthal, P. R., 28

Lynda.com, 104, 105

M

Maintenance, course, 185–186

Managing Online Education survey (Green), xviii

Manning, S., 123, 124, 134, 167, 168

Marczynsk, K., 28

Marx, D. B., xviii

MIT OpenCourseware, 95

Materials. *See* Instructional materials

Math practice activities, 119–120

Mayer, R. E., 98–101

McTighe, J., 14–15

Measurability, of learning outcomes, 48, 49

Meloni, C., 166

Memory, continuity principle and, 99–100

Mental images, 97–98

Merlot.org, 102, 119–120, 122

Metacognition, 37, 39–40, 81

Metacognitive scaffolding, 87, 88, 123, 179

Metzner, B., 6–7, 24–25, 28, 81

Microsoft Movie Maker, 104, 106

Microsoft Office, 42, 103

Microsoft Outlook, 169

Microsoft Viseo, 104, 106

Microsoft Word, 42

Midterm exam, 55

Miller, G. A., 100

Mills, M. E., xvii

Miniature Guide to Critical Thinking (Paul and Elder), 93

Minute papers, 180

Miszkiewics, M. J., 28

Monitoring tools, 179

Monterey Institute for Technology and Education, 9

Moreno, R., 98–101

Motivation: active learning and, 81; cognitive scaffolding and, 86; in deep *versus* surface learning, 6; discussion and, 125; formative assessments for, 61–62; of online learners, 24; in problem-based learning, 133; synchronous communication and, 166

Muddiest point discussions, 126, 180

Multimedia: benefits of, 96; creation of, 103–106; criteria for, 108; functional requirements of, 113; maintenance of, 185–186; for personal introductions, 155; process for selecting, 101–106; resources and software for, 101–106; software for, 103–106; theories and principles of, 98–101; types of, 96–98

Multimedia Educational Resource for Learning and Online Teaching (MERLOT), 102, 119–120, 122

Multiple perspectives, discussion for, 124–130

Multiple representation, 98, 99

Museums, 97

N

National Gallery of Art, 97

National Online Learners Priorities Report (Noel-Levitz), 24

National Public Radio (NPR), 102

Navigation: clear reverse in, 163; consistent logic in, 163, 165; design principles for, 162–164; importance of, 161–162; landmarks in, 164; obvious start in, 162–163; proximity of elements in, 164; standard practice conventions in, 164

Navigation bar, 154, 162–163

Needs analysis, learner, 23, 29–31

Negative path, 6

News-based discussion, 126

Noel-Levitz, 24

If you enjoyed this book, you may also like these:

**Effective Online Teaching
by Tina Stavredes**
ISBN: 9780470578384

**Effective Online Teaching
Training Manual
by Tina Stavredes**
ISBN: 9780470578391

WILEY